Canada   Pictures of a Great Land

Canada

Pictures of a Great Land

Produced by Jürgen F. Boden and Hans Scherz

GAGE PUBLISHING

Gage Publishing

© 1976 by Jürgen F. Boden and Hans Scherz

All rights reserved. No part of this book may be reproduced

in any form without permission in writing from the publisher

ISBN: 0-7715-9330-9

Published simultaneously in the Federal Republic of Germany by

Umschau Verlag Breidenstein KG, Frankfurt am Main

and in France by Editions Vilo, Paris

Printed and bound in Germany by

Brönners Druckerei Breidenstein KG, Frankfurt am Main

Authors

Text

Pierre Berton
Jean-Louis Gagnon
A. E. Johann

Poems

Duke Redbird
Alootook Ipellie

Translations

E. L. B. Languages Group,
London

Layout

Hans Scherz

Photographers

Peter d'Angelo
Paul von Baich
Jen & Des Bartlett
Erich Baumann
Hans Blohm
Egon Bork
Bill Brooks
Fred Bruemmer
George Brybycin
Alma H. Carmichael
Albert J. Carter
Marc Ellefsen
Ken Elliott
Hälle Flygare
John Foster
Ted Grant
Rudi Haas
Tom Hall
George Harris
Phil Hersee
Bert Hoferichter
George Hunter
Colin Irwin
Peter Kelly
Hendrik Kiliaan
J. A. Kraulis
Ulrich Kretschmar

John Launois
Gar Lunney
Peter Mackinnon
Mia & Klaus
John R. Murray
Don Newlands
Barry Ranford
Leonard Lee Rue III
D. W. Schmidt
Ted Spiegel
Boris Spremo
Peter Thomas
John de Visser
Richard Vroom
C. M. Young

Acknowledgements

The producers of this book wish to express their gratitude toward the many Canadian photographers who generously submitted their work and time to us. Through their personal interpretations we have been able to present to an international audience a complete mosaic of Canada. We would also like to thank the National Film Board of Canada for their assistance and co-operation.
Of no less importance to this book are the essays and poems complementing the pictorial portrait. They have been written with profound knowledge and deep feeling for a great land, and we wish to thank the authors.

Jürgen F. Boden   Hans Scherz

Contents

Aspects of Canada

The Parliament Buildings in Ottawa, Canada's capital, are a dignified landmark of sober Victorian architecture.

Les bâtiments du Parlement à Ottawa, capitale du Canada, monument sobre et digne, caractéristique de l'architecture victorienne.

Ottawa, Parlamentsgebäude. Das Wahrzeichen der kanadischen Bundeshauptstadt ist ein Monument traditionell-englischen Baustils.

▷
Canada's thoroughfares and buildings are as generous and gigantic as the country itself. Left: Hwy. 401 at Toronto, main arterial road between the Quebec borders and Windsor, Ontario.   Right: The CN Tower against Toronto's skyline, at 1815 feet the highest free-standing structure in the world.

Les voies de communication et les immeubles du Canada sont à l'instar du pays: gigantesques et généreux.   A gauche: la grande route 401, principale voie de communication reliant Montréal et Windsor.   A droite: le gratte-ciel CN de Toronto. la plus haute tour du monde avec ses 1801 pieds.

Großzügig und gigantisch wie das Land selbst sind die von seinen Menschen geschaffenen Verkehrswege und Bauwerke.
Links: Autostraße Nr. 401, Hauptverbindung zwischen Montreal und Windsor, Ontario. Rechts: Der CN-Tower im Stadtbild von Toronto, mit 553 Metern höchster Turm der Welt.

▷▷
Canada is just about the last of the world's countries to offer a new home and ample opportunities to many of the races and nationalities shown here on Ottawa's Sparks Street Mall.

Le Canada est l'un des derniers pays à offrir d'immenses possibilités à chacun, quelle que soit sa race ou sa nationalité. Scène de la vie quotidienne dans la Sparks Street Mall, paradis des piétons dans le quartier d'affaires d'Ottawa.

Kanada, Land der immer noch fast unbegrenzten Möglichkeiten für Menschen aller Rassen und Nationalitäten. Alltagsszenen auf der Sparks Street Mall, dem Fußgängerparadies im Geschäftsviertel von Ottawa.

Ice hockey, the sport invented in Canada is both played and watched with passionate enthusiasm. Below: Team Canada vs. USSR.

Le hockey sur glace est depuis toujours le sport le plus pratiqué au pays des nombreux lacs et des hivers rigoureux. Ci-dessous: rencontre internationale Canada–URSS.

Eishockey ist im Land der vielen Seen und strengen Winter seit jeher Volkssport Nummer eins. Unten: Kanada – UdSSR.

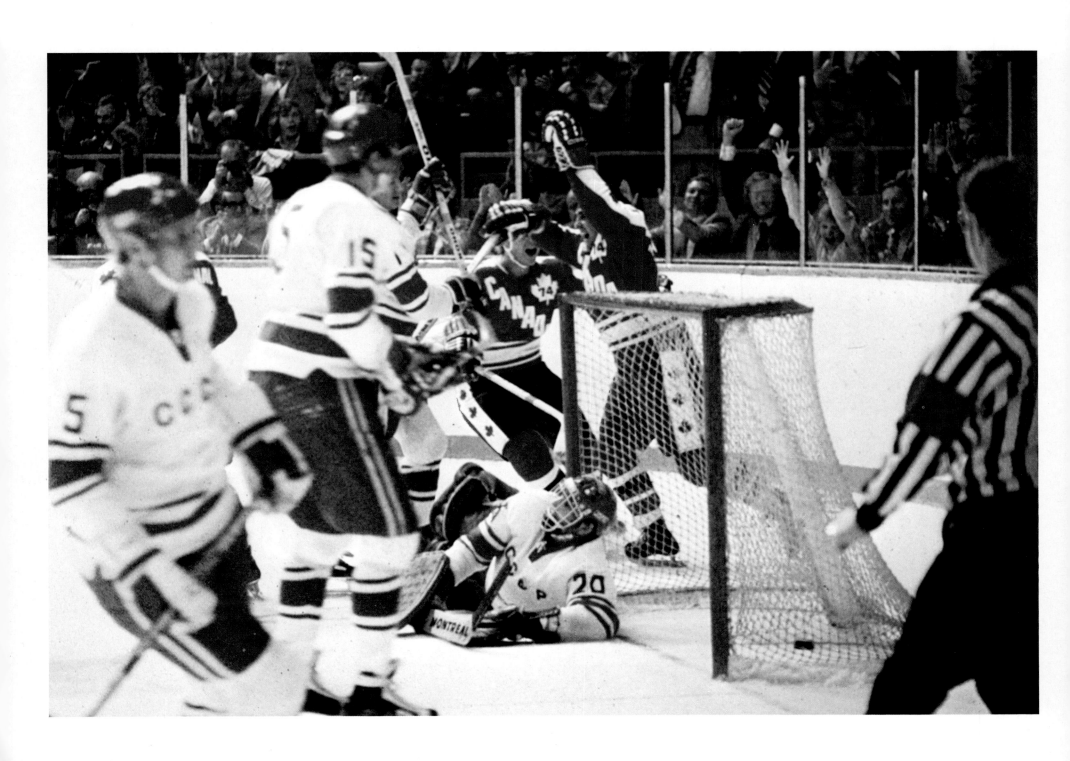

The 27-mile Welland Canal links Lake Ontario with Lake Erie, 7 locks for a total lift of 320 feet. A special North American "laker" vessel carries cargoes of 25,000 tons of iron or 1,000,000 bushels of grain through this important gateway.

Le canal Welland de 27 miles de longueur, relie le lac Ontario au lac Erié. 7 écluses pour une hauteur de chute totale de 320 pieds. Des cargots de grains et de minerais, pouvant peser jusqu'à 25 000 tonnes, passent par cette importante voie.

Der Welland-Kanal, 43 Kilometer lang und mit 7 Schleusen ausgestattet, verbindet den St. Lorenzstrom über den Ontario See mit den anderen Großen Seen und schafft damit die Schiffsverbindung bis hin nach Thunder Bay, Provinz Manitoba.

◁

A steel mill at Oshawa, Ontario where a highly developed industry draws the needed raw materials out of Canada's immense treasure of natural resources.

Une industrie hautement développée tire ses besoins en matières premières de l'immense trésor de ressources naturelles. Sur notre photo: une aciérie à Oshawa dans l'Ontario.

Aus den unermeßlich reichen Bodenschätzen des Landes schöpft eine hochentwickelte Industrie ihre Rohstoffe. Unser Bild: Stahlwerk in Oshawa, Provinz Ontario.

The Chateau Frontenac, one of Canada's
grand hotels perched on Cape Diamond
overlooking the St. Lawrence River in Quebec
where it was erected at the end of the last
century. Still the cultural centre of French
Canada, Quebec is the only walled city in
North America and the oldest city in Canada.

Le Château Frontenac, l'un des plus
grands hôtels du Canada, a été construit à la
fin du siècle dernier. Perché sur le Cap
Diamant, il surplombe le St-Laurent.
Québec, la plus ancienne ville du Canada,
aujourd'hui encore centre culturel du Canada
français, est la seule ville fortifiée d'Amérique
du Nord.

Quebec. Grand Hotel Château Frontenac
(erbaut im 19. Jahrhundert) thront auf einem
Felsen über dem St. Lorenzstrom. Von hier
blickt man auf Häuser und Stadtmauern
dieser ältesten kanadischen Stadt. Quebec
ist noch heute kultureller Mittelpunkt
Französisch-Kanadas.

Pierre Berton   My Country

To a stranger, the land must seem endless.
A herring gull, winging its way west from St. John's on the eastern spur of Newfoundland to Victoria on the southern tip of Vancouver Island will travel as far as the distance from London to Baghdad. It is this vastness that beggars the imagination of all who visit my country.

The tattered Atlantic coastline, with its sombre cliffs, its raging tidal bore and its picture postcard harbors, gives way, as we move inland to the wooded coves and habitant strip farms of the St. Lawrence valley. The great river is almost four thousand kilometres long and to the north of it one can see the Laurentian hills, sandpapered to a woman's roundness by the erosion of time. Beyond those hills lies the bleak wilderness of Labrador, which an early explorer called "the land God gave to Cain."

The river spills out of that chain of inland seas we call the Great Lakes, deep in Canada's industrial heartland. These lakes (there are four of them in Canada) stretch for more than twelve hundred kilometres, as the gull flies, along the American border – vast depressions gouged by the Pleistocene glaciers from the timeless pre-Cambrian rock of the Laurentian Shield. It is sobering to realize that far off to the north, some three thousand kilometres distant, in the land of the Yellowknife and Dogrib Indians, two equally immense lakes lie cradled in this same unbroken desert of rock.

But we are still travelling directly west. Beyond the tip of Lake Superior we encounter that Canadian phenomenon, the muskeg – a 500 kilometre stretch of scrub forest and frozen swampland. In these frigid bogs in the late nineteenth century entire locomotives vanished without a trace, be-devilling the early railroad builders.

Beyond the muskeg country the prairies stretch off toward the Rockies for 1500 kilometres. To the early explorers the first sight of these plains was almost as awesome as the first view of the snow-clad peaks that mark their western boundary. As little as a century ago they were still in their virgin state – a seemingly endless ocean of waist high grass, utterly treeless, flat as a hockey rink, a "great, boundless solitary wast of verdure" in the words of William Francis Butler, the explorer who crossed them in 1870. Butler called this country The Great Lone Land, but it is lonely no longer, having been shaved, ploughed, planted and fenced by a succession of settlers who transformed it into the world's breadbasket. Pekinese and Muscovites are nurtured today on the provender of these wheatfields.

The plains give way, finally, to the rolling foothills of Alberta; beyond those hills a jagged wall of mountains meets the eye. This alpine rampart, eight hundred kilometres thick, is really a series of granite and sandstone walls, riven by alluvial action and separated by vast trenches that run north and south, draining the glacier-fed land. Beyond the mountains lie the dense rain forests and glittering fiords of the Pacific coast and the ragged islands that mark the western extremities of my country.

That is the Canada the train traveller encounters as he steams westward on a journey that takes the best part of a week; but it is only a slice of the whole. My country is half as thick as it is broad: It is almost twice as deep as the United States and considerably deeper than either China or the Soviet Union. Only a determined few have been able to travel the immense northern waterways, the Yukon and Mackenzie, which flow north to the Arctic, or to venture out in that chill desert we call the Barren Ground, or to visit the bald islands in the frozen ocean or to fly across the navy blue expanse of Hudson Bay, where the freezing waters act as a continental thermostat.

Only a minority of my countrymen have been able to view these wonders. Contrary to universal belief, we do not live in snow-covered cabins far from civilization. Most of us are hived in cities that do not seem, at first glance to differ greatly from those to the south of us. The perceptive visitor, however, will note some differences. We are not a homogenous people and the ethnicity of our makeup is, I believe, more pronounced than it is in the melting pot to the south. A newcomer in the United States quickly learns to submerge his origins and become an American. A newcomer to Canada manages to retain something of his ethnic background.

If we are officially bilingual we are also unofficially multicultural. That original decision to allow the conquered French settlers to retain their own language, culture and religion, has had some effect on all cultures and religions. It is said, for instance, that there is more Gaelic spoken on Cape Breton Island in Nova Scotia than there is in Scotland. For the same reasons, there are men and women in the former British colony of Victoria, on Vancouver Island, who continue to speak with an English accent even though they were born in Canada. I knew some of them when I lived there in the thirties; and at that point Victoria had been a part of Canada for more than 60 years.

Some of the history of Canada can be divined from its customs and its place names. The country was invaded from both coasts. The French, the Portuguese, the Scots, and the English were the first to reach the Atlantic Coast (if one excepts those temporary residents, the Norsemen of Iceland). That influx began at the end of the fifteenth century. Long before that Mongolian nomads had crossed the Bering ice bridge between Siberia and Alaska to filter down the coast and into the interior to father the native tribes of Indians and Inuit who were the first Canadians. It was the Eskimos of Baffin Island who greeted the first Elizabethan explorers in 1576 and the Haidas, Nootkas and Kwakiutls who encountered the original Spaniards and the English when they reached the Pacific coastline in the seventeenth century.

Since then the immigrant tide has never ebbed as the place names and customs of my country suggest. The accents of the Newfoundland fishermen are the most distinctive in Canada and hark back to Elizabethan times. Portuguese seamen, seeking plunder on the Grand Banks, still roam the streets of St. John's as they have for some four hundred years. Men and women proudly wear the kilt in Nova Scotia, while in neighbouring New Brunswick, the land of the Acadians and Longfellow's poem *Evangeline,* French is heard almost as often as English.

The Tremblays of the Saguenay valley in Quebec (who speak with a different accent than the Acadians) can trace their lineage back to the days of the Sun King. In British Ontario, there is scarcely a town that does not have its King, Princess, Duke and Duchess Street, its Royal Cafe and its Queen's Hotel. In the ivy-covered Empress Hotel of Victoria, four o'clock tea, in the English fashion, is an afternoon ritual. But the bays and the islands that surround the town, not to mention the avenues, tend to bear names like Gonzales, Quadra, Galiano and Valdez.

The heartland of my country was, naturally enough, the last to be settled. For centuries, the plains and forest of central Canada knew only the French and Scottish fur traders – *coureurs de bois* and *voyageurs.* The ethnic mix of the prairies is totally different because of the waves of Eastern Europeans, "the men in sheepskin coats," who poured in during the first decade of the present century. One can still see the *babushka* worn in Manitoba while the onion-shaped profile of the Ukrainian churches is as familiar on the skyline as that of the grain elevator. Places like Gimli (Icelandic), and Esterhazy (Hungarian) dot the wheatlands, along with those settlements that bear such indigenous titles as Cut Knife, Elkhorn and Yellow Grass.

In our cities, since the end of World War II we have become accustomed to a new mosaic of cultures brought about by post-war immigration. Robson street in Vancouver has been nicknamed *Robsonstrasse* because the shops, delicatessens and cafes that run for several blocks are all European. Toronto's little Italy, with a population exceeding 300,000, is a city within a city – the largest of its kind on the continent. Before 1950 few Canadians had tasted espresso, borscht, goulash, schnitzel, pizza, won ton, tempura, sachertorte, paella, shishkabab, fondue or sauerbraten; today they are almost as familiar as beef and potatoes or pork and beans. The Toronto telephone directory lists its foreign restaurants under 33 separate categories from Arabian to Ukrainian.

There is even now a native northwest Indian restaurant in Vancouver, serving traditional West Coast Indian dishes. The native peoples, so long deprived of their culture, are again a force to be reckoned within my country. The slogan "red power" is a vague one, meaning many things: a pride in race, a new militancy, a determination to retain a distinctive identity, an insistence on an aboriginal right to certain lands, and the resurgence of a culture that was once despised, then forgotten and is now much admired.

The Inuit, perhaps because they have been more isolated than the Indians from white influence, have not only managed to retain much of their artistry; they have also built upon it. The boom in Eskimo art – both sculpture and print-making – is one of the unforeseen phenomena of our time. Deprived by the march of civilization of the nomadic hunters' existence, the Inuit, through their co-operatives, are reaping the benefit of that boom. A personal example suggests its dimensions: a small Eskimo print that I purchased in 1962 for $35 was valued in 1975 at $1,000.

Traditionally, the stranger has thought of Canada as a land of Indians and Eskimos, interspersed with French-Canadian trappers and red-coated Mounted Policemen, braving snowswept wastes and tall, glacier-topped mountains. It comes as a surprise to many to learn that there are hundreds of thousands of us who have never seen an Eskimo, and some who have not even seen an Indian, a mountain or a Mountie. Most of us, as I have said, are city folk. Village life is fast declining. In southern Ontario you will find scores of grave-yards that are the only evidence of vanished communities. On the prairies, there are hundreds of once thriving settlements transformed into ghost towns. New farming methods, modern transportation, the decline of the railways, the centralization of industry – all these have had their effect on rural life.

Contrary to popular myth, Mounties rarely wear scarlet coats in my country. Indians look very much like the rest of us, in their cloth caps and wool shirts, except that they are poorer. Eskimos live far away in the north where they drive snow-mobiles, not dogteams, and motorboats rather than kayaks. To see the Rockies most Canadians must travel for hundreds of miles and pay an equal number of dollars. Most can't afford it. Certainly it can get very cold in Canada. Few Europeans understand that it can also get very hot. At Fort Smith, in the North West Territories, the temperature has risen as high as 40 °C. In the Yukon, where I was born and raised, I have worked in tropical conditions hacking survey lines through a jungle-like growth with a native machete. The Eastern cities swelter in the humidity of July and August and people actually die each year of heat prostration. Honolulu, for instance, has never known the highs of Montreal. In Victoria, roses and wall flowers bloom on Christmas day and the golf courses are open twelve months a year. But, of course, we Canadians also know what it is like to be cold. In 1947, when the ther-mometer dropped to minus 65 °C at a place called Snag in the Yukon, it was so cold that men left vapour trails behind them when they moved and a bucket of water tossed into the air, fell to the ground as ice.

Where temperature is concerned we are a country of extremes; and yet, as a people, we tend toward moderation and even conservatism. Europeans tend to lump us together with our American neigh-bours but we are not really like the Americans. Our temperament, our social attitudes, our environment and our history make us a different kind of North American. Though these differences may not be easy for a newcomer to understand, they are very real to us.

First, there is the matter of our history. It has been called dull, by which it is generally meant that it is not very bloody. Certainly we have no strong tradition of violence in our first century as an independent nation. We are, after all, the only people in all the Americas who did not separate violently from Europe. We have had three or four picayune uprisings but nothing that could be called a revolution or a civil war. No matter what the movies tell you, we had no wild west and no wild Indians. Personal weaponry is not our style: No Canadian feels he has an inalienable right to carry a gun. Lynchings, vigilante groups and shoot-outs are unknown in our past and in our present. The Mounted Police were invented not to fight the Indians but to prevent white renegades from the United States from demoralizing the Indians. Our two great gold rushes, the first to central British Columbia and the second to the storied Klondike, were so carefully policed that there is little record of bloodshed. In Dawson City in 1898 – the peak year of the great stampede – there wasn't a single murder or major theft. The worst crimes were typically Canadian ones:

breaking the Sabbath laws; conducting an obscene performance in the theatre. We have been, and to a considerable extent remain, a Puritan people.

There are several reasons for this bloodlessness, which differs markedly from the histories of the other European colonies on both the American continents. First, there was the presence of those people who refused to fight against England during the American Revolution and who came, instead, to Canada, at great personal sacrifice. The influence of these United Empire Loyalists (my ancestor, Peter Berton, was one) has been far out of proportion to their numbers. The Americans called them Tories, and that is certainly what they were – conservatives to the death. Together with that other influential minority group, the Scots, who controlled the banks, railways and educational institutions, they have helped give us our reputation as a canny, cautious, provident people. It is no accident that Canadians have the highest rate of bank and insurance savings in the world. To a large extent it has been the American entre-preneurs who have taken the financial risks in my country – and that explains why so much of Canada's manufacturing, industry and natural resources are American owned or controlled.

We were slow to shed our colonial shackles. While the Americans opted for freedom (and some-times, on the frontier, for anarchy) we opted for order. Our lawmen are appointed from above, not elected from below. The idea of choosing town marshalls and county sheriffs by ballot to keep the peace with six-shooters never fitted into the Canadian scheme of things. Instead, in the first days of our new nationhood, we invented the North West Mounted Police who did not depend on votes to stay in power. The Canadian symbol of the Mountie, impeccable in his scarlet coat, clashes with the American symbol of the shaggy lawman in his open shirt and gunbelt. The two differing social attitudes persist to this day.

In the United States, for geographical reasons as well as social ones, the settlers moved across the continent before the law – hence the "wild" west. In Canada the law came first; settlement followed. Saloons were unknown on the Canadian prairies. So were gambling halls, gunmen and Indian massacres.

Outward displays of emotion are not part of the Canadian style. In spite of what I have written about heat waves, we are, after all, a northern people, with the phlegmatic qualities that one associates with Scotsmen and Swedes. We do not live in the streets as southern races do. We are an interior people in more ways than one. The Americans are far more outgoing than we are. One reason for this, I think, is the very real presence of nature in our lives. Although it is true that we are city folk, most of us live within a few hours' drive of the wilderness. We escape to the woods whenever we can. Montrealers head for the Laurentian mountains on weekends; Torontonians to the lakes of Muskoka and Haliburton. Calgarians move into the Rockies; Vancouverites into the rain forests of the coast. No Canadian city is far removed from those mysterious and silent places which can have such an effect on the human soul.

It is no accident that we have saved our cultural applause – it amounts, almost, to reverence – for the one school of painting that showed us something of that wilderness. The oil sketches of the Group of Seven depicting the gnarled schists and gneisses of the Shield, the wind-tattered pines, the gunmetal lakes and the stark Arctic islands, are familiar to every schoolchild. One of the most famous of these paintings is called *The Solemn Land*. It does not show the Canada of the tourist posters but a different Canada, one that every Canadian but few Europeans know – dark and brooding, bereft of colour, empty and silent. Almost every Canadian sometime in his life has heard the haunting call of the loon and the lonely call of the wolf and seen the skeletal birches limned against the dun-colored sky and felt "that shiver of awe and loneliness which comes to a man when he stands alone in the face of untamed Nature".

There is another aspect of my country that makes it unique in the Americas and that is our bilingual and bicultural makeup. It gives us a picturesque quality, of course, and that is certainly a tourist asset: visitors are as intrigued by the "foreigness" of Quebec City, with its twisting streets and its habitant atmosphere, as they are by the high standard of French cuisine in Montreal. But there is also a disturbing regional tension. We are, in an official phrase coined a century and a half ago, "two nations warring in the bosom of a single state." And this has affected us all.

Quebec has become a nation within a nation. Each of Canada's ten provinces are, supposedly, equal; but Quebec is a province unlike any other. This is as much a matter of religion and culture as it is of language; the twin spires of the Roman Catholic churches, until recently the most powerful influence in French Canadian life, still dominate the horizons of *la belle province*. More influential today are the popular songs, the stage plays, the novels, films, television and radio shows, few of which are ever translated into English and thus remain unknown to most other Canadians.

This *de facto* separation of Quebec, political now as well as cultural, and the federal government's strenuous efforts to prevent it from becoming *de jure,* has exacerbated the historic regional tensions which have always existed in other parts of Canada. We are, after all, a young country, politically speaking. Canadians still tend to think of themselves in narrow provincial terms. Newfoundlanders, who only became Canadians in 1948, still talk of "Mainlanders" as if they were citizens of a different nation, as Victorians once referred to politicians from Eastern Canada as "white Chinamen" (i. e. foreign interlopers). The residents of three Maritime provinces (Prince Edward Island, Nova Scotia and New Brunswick) continue to speak disparagingly of "Upper Canadians," a phrase that was made obsolete when the province of Ontario was created by the Confederation of 1867. The country is further divided into The West and The East, the boundary line being the Manitoba-Ontario border. The West is as suspicious and as jealous of The East as the Maritimes are of Upper Canada. Alberta indeed has a small separatist party; it does not amount to much at the moment, but one must remember that twenty years ago the Quebec separatist movement was equally ineffective.

All the same, it may be true, as one political analyst has recently argued, that it is these very tensions that help to give Canada a distinct identity, that "Canadian civilization . . . has . . . produced by the force of its contradictions a distinctive economic culture and a distinctive artistic culture – a singular Canadian way of life . . ."

Quebec's struggle to maintain a cultural identity in an English-speaking ocean is a microcosm of a similar struggle by the nation as a whole to maintain a distinctive identity in a predominantly American milieu. French Canada's resistance to English Canada's cultural and economic pressure can be seen to parallel English Canada's resistance to the same kind of pressure from the United States. In this curious paradox can be found the essence of being a Canadian. It helps explain why those English-speaking Canadians who call themselves nationalists are among the most fervent supporters of a special status for the province of Quebec.

Our politics, our economic system, our social attitudes and to a considerable extent our national character are all products of our reaction and our resistance to the blandishments that come from the south of the border. We are beginning to realize that we are becoming, essentially, a public enterprise country in contrast to the private enterprise country below our borders. And that public enterprise, which manifested itself first in a canal system and later in railways, hydro projects and airlines, and which has spilled over into broadcasting, films, utilities, communications satellites and an entire galaxy of Crown corporations (which account for one-third of all Canadian-controlled corporate assets) – that public enterprise has almost always come about as part of our response to the United States.

Our first transcontinental railway was built, largely with public funds, to stitch the country together and prevent an American takeover of the Canadian northwest. Later railways all fell into government hands. The Canadian Film Development Corporation, the National Film Board, the Canadian Broadcasting Corporation, the Canada Council – all were devised to support Canadian culture against foreign incursion. We have had little choice in the matter. In order to counter the flood of motion pictures, TV programs, magazines, books, and above all, investment that pours across the border we have been forced to create a new kind of economic system, that differs markedly from the free-wheeling competitive system to the south. The establishment of the Canadian Development Corporation, another publicly-owned company designed to buy back bits of Canada from American owners, is only the most recent in a century-long series of political decisions intended to prevent Canada from becoming an economic satellite of a foreign country.

This is not to suggest that Canadians are anti-American. If anything, the opposite is true. We watch the American television offerings avidly (some complain more avidly, than we watch our own). We read the American magazines, the American comic strips, the American columnists and the American best-selling novels. We tend to prefer American-made cars over the European and Asian products, although that may be changing. We watch the American political conventions with at least the same excitement with which we view our own. We welcome hundreds of thousands of American tourists to our country every year and only wince slightly when they tell us that we're exactly the same as they are.

Of course we're *not* the same. But the visitor may be pardoned for thinking so when he first crosses the border. The buildings in our cities are designed in the international styles of Le Corbusier and Mies van der Rohe. The brand names in the supermarkets are all familiar. The chicken palaces, hot dog stands, gas stations and motels that line our superhighways are American-franchised operations. It is only after several days that the newcomer begins to sense a difference – subtle at first, and then, perhaps, more pronounced. He cannot put his finger on that difference but then, neither can many of my countrymen. The only thing we are really sure of is that we are not Americans.

It is only since our centennial year of 1967 that we have begun to try to define the Canadian character. Our hundredth birthday provided an injection of confidence. After all, in spite of all the pulls and tensions, we were still united. We had mounted a successful world exhibition in Montreal, using all the flair of the Quebecois and all the organizing ability of the English-Canadians. We began then to learn a little about ourselves and to remember a little more about ourselves.

Being a Canadian is compounded of a variety of

odd items that are totally familiar only to a Canadian. The school hockey rink is one and the Laurentian Shield – that pockmarked desert of rock that covers two-fifths of my country, is another. All of us bask in the knowledge that our first Prime Minister mixed gin with his drinking water during public debates and that our most durable was a spiritualist who believed himself in contact with his deceased mother. Our heroes include a rebel, Louis Riel, hanged for treason, a hockey star, Bobby Orr, who plays for a team in Boston, and a railway builder, William Van Horne, who was born in Michigan, U. S. A. Every Canadian knows of an intoxicating drink called "screech," which is sold only in Newfoundland and even non-football fans watch the Grey Cup game in November, a national rite that bids fair to overshadow the traditional Stanley Cup hockey playoffs in the spring. Almost every Canadian is familiar with the Calgary Stampede, a rodeo that takes place in southern Alberta in July and the Klondike Days which are held in nearby Edmonton about the same time, some 1500 miles southeast of the real Klondike. These are the things that unite us, along with the paintings of Tom Thomson, our mythic artist, drowned mysteriously (and aptly, a foreign observer might say) in a canoe in the wilderness. For better or for worse all this belongs to us and to nobody else, like the CPR and the CBC, the CIC and the CLC – a meaningless jumble of letters to a stranger but as familiar to most of us as maple syrup, all of them standing for a special kind of Canadian institution specifically designed (along with scores of others) for the purpose of maintaining my country as a small but spirited independent nation, unique in the American hemisphere.

Eastern Canada

Quebec Winter Carnival: the pièce de résistance is the canoe race across the ice-choked St. Lawrence River.

Le Carnaval d'hiver de Québec: le clou de cette fête est la course en canoë à travers le St. Laurent obstrué de glace, une épreuve pour des hommes authentiques.

Sport nur für harte Männer. Höhepunkt des Winterkarnevals von Quebec ist das Kanu-Rennen über den eisschollenbedeckten St. Lorenzstrom.

Peggy's Cove on Nova Scotia's Atlantic shores; one of the many dreamy yet busy fishing villages of the 4 historic Maritime provinces.

Peggy's Cove, l'un des nombreux villages de pêcheurs au cadre enchanteur sur le littoral atlantique de la Nouvelle-Ecosse. Au large de Terre-Neuve, la Nouvelle-Ecosse est l'une des provinces maritimes, avec le Nouveau-Brunswick et l'Ile du Prince Edouard, qui jouèrent un rôle important lors de la fondation du Canada.

Peggy's Cove, einer der vielen Fischereihäfen an der Atlantik-Küste von Nova Scotia. Neuschottland gehört neben Neufundland, Neubraunschweig und der Prinz-Edward-Insel zu den vier „Maritime"-Provinzen im Osten, die in der Gründerzeit Kanadas Geschichte machten.

The beaver, symbol of Canada, once the animal most hunted by Indians and trappers for his pelt. The fur trade operated by the Hudson's Bay Company and the North West Company made important contributions toward the exploration and development of Canada.

Le castor, symbole du Canada, était autrefois l'animal le plus recherché par les Indiens et les trappeurs. Le commerce de la fourrure par la Hudson's Bay Company et la North West Company contribua beaucoup à l'ouverture et au développement du Canada.

Der Biber, Symbolfigur für Kanada, war einst begehrtestes Beutetier der Indianer und Trapper. Jagd und Pelzhandel führten zur raschen Erschließung des Landes durch die Hudson's Bay Company und die North West Company.

A heavy storm threatens the
rugged coast line in the Bay of
Fundy over Nova Scotia's Cape
Split – a name that brings to mind
a vision of waves smashing
against the cracking beams of
sailing ships.

Une forte tempête sur le Cap Split,
un nom qui fait penser au
craquement des poutres de
bateaux et au fracas des vagues
déferlant sur cette côte
accidentée et sauvage de la Baie
de Fundy en Nouvelle-Ecosse.

„Cape Split" – ein Name, der an
krachende Wogen und an
splitternde Schiffsbalken denken
läßt. Hier schlagen die Wellen an
die steil aufragende Felsküste von
Neuschottland.

Ottawa Valley, north of Canada's capital in the province of Quebec, where the gentle agricultural land dotted with family farms is subtly reminiscent of Europe. Below: An Indian father and child take a little time out from farm chores.

La vallée de l'Outaouais dans la province de Québec. Les fermes familiales de style européen s'intégrent harmonieusement dans la beauté du paysage. Ci-dessous, un Indien et son enfant se reposant des travaux de la ferme.

Ottawa Valley, Provinz Quebec. In einer europäisch anmutenden Landschaft liegen Kleinfarmen. Unten: Ein indianischer Landarbeiter ruht sich mit seinem Kind von der Arbeit aus.

The charming metropolis of Montreal, pulsating monument to the economic and cultural co-existence of the two great cultures in Canada, is the second largest French-speaking city in the world (next to Paris). With more than 2.8 million people, Canada's largest city also has large ambitions: 1967 – EXPO, the world exhibition, 1976 – Olympic Summer Games.

Le charme de Montréal sur le St-Laurent, métropole du Canada et seconde ville de langue française du monde après Paris, avec plus de 2,8 millions d'habitants. Exemple stimulateur de la co-existence culturelle et économique des deux grandes cultures du pays. Une ville aux grandes ambitions: l'exposition internationale en 1967, les 21èmes Jeux Olympiques d'Eté en 1976.

Weltstadt Montreal (2,8 Mill. Einwohner). Blick vom Mont Royal auf die Stadt und den St. Lorenz-Strom. Montreal, Beweis wirtschaftlicher und kultureller Koexistenz der beiden großen Kulturen Kanadas und pulsierende Metropole der Provinz Quebec, veranstaltete 1967 die Weltausstellung. 1976 ist Montreal Austragungsort der XXI. Olympischen Sommer-Spiele.

In the last decades Canada has developed its own precision industries with products exported around the world. Shown here: Optical plant in Midland, Ontario.

Au cours des dernières décennies, le Canada a développé ses propres industries de précision et ses produits sont exportés dans le monde entier. Sur la photo: une usine d'instruments d'optique dans le Midland, Ontario.

Kanada hat in den letzten Jahrzehnten eine eigene Präzisionsindustrie aufgebaut, deren Erzeugnisse in alle Welt exportiert werden. Unser Bild: Optische Werke in Midland, Provinz Ontario.

▷
Left: Old and new skyscrapers in the centre of dynamic, fast-growing Toronto, second largest city in Canada with 2.7 million people and the country's centre of industry and commerce. Right: Montreal's Metro system has some of the world's most attractive stations.

A gauche, des gratte-ciel du centre de Toronto, ville à la croissance rapide et dynamique, et seconde ville du Canada avec plus de 2,7 millions d'habitants. C'est un centre industriel et commercial. A droite, le métro de Montréal.

Links: Alte und neue „Sky-Scrapers" im Stadtbild von Toronto. Kanadas zweitgrößte und dynamisch wachsende Stadt (2,7 Mill. Einwohner), ist Verwaltungsmetropole für Industrie und Banken. Rechts: Metro-Station in Montreal.

FRANK'S

HAMBURGERS

Two faces of Canada: a smiling French-Canadian construction worker and a lovely freckled girl of English descent.

Deux générations de Canadiens: un ouvrier du bâtiment souriant, Canadien français, et une charmante jeune fille pleine de taches de rousseur, de descendance anglaise.

Kanadier aus zwei Generationen. Die Abstammung ist unverkennbar. Bild links: Franko-kanadischer Bauarbeiter. Bild rechts: Schülerin englischer Abstammung.

Hydro Quebec's Manicouagan-Outardes
project will produce upon completion
5.540.000 kw. on the two rivers north of Baie
Comeau at the upper St. Lawrence River. One
of several hydro-electric power plants in
Quebec, this province is the richest in water-
power resources in Canada and the largest
exporter to its southern neighbor.

Le projet hydraulique de Manicouagan-
Outardes de Québec en cours de réalisation,
qui produira 5 540 000 kwt sur les deux
rivières au nord de la Baie Comeau,
au-dessus du fleuve St-Laurent. Une des
nombreuses usines hydroélectriques, et le
plus grand exportateur d'électricité vers le
voisin du Sud.

Der Manic-Staudamm, nördlich vom Baie
Comeau am Oberlauf des St. Lorenzstromes
gelegen, ist nur einer von vielen Super-
Staudämmen in Kanada. Das Manicouagan-
Outardes-Projekt, mit der größten Bogen-
mauer der Welt und einer Kapazität von über
5,5 Millionen Kilowatt, versorgt auch den
Nachbarn USA mit elektrischer Energie.

Canada has tens of thousands of rivers and lakes with clean waters and an abundance of fish. Below: fishing is one of the weekend highlights for young and old Canadians in the vicinity of Ontario's Algonquin Provincial Park. Right: whistling swans on their fall migration from Canada to the south.

Le Canada, semé de forêts, foisonnant d'une multitude de lacs et de rivières aux eaux limpides et poissonneuses, est un paradis où la nature respectée rayonne dans sa beauté originelle. La pêche est l'un des passe-temps favoris des jeunes et des vieux. Ci-dessous des pêcheurs dans le parc provincial Algonquin en Ontario. A droite: vol migratoire des cygnes chanteurs vers le sud.

In Kanada findet jeder noch ein Stück unberührter Natur, denn unermeßlich sind Wälder, Seen und Flüsse im zweitgrößten Land der Erde. Unten: Angeln, beliebtes Freizeitvergnügen für Jung und Alt. Rechts: Schwäne auf ihrem Herbstzug nach dem Süden.

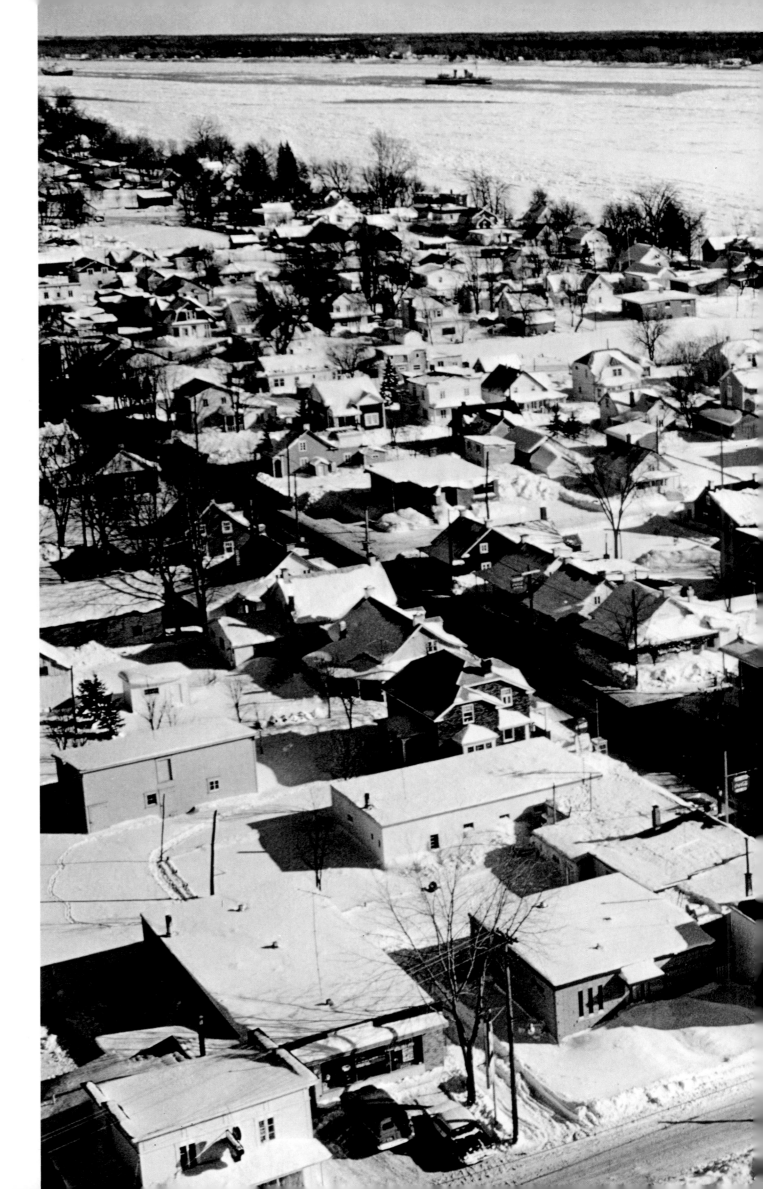

A typical French-Canadian village on the banks of the ice-covered St. Lawrence River between Montreal and Quebec.

Un village canadien-français typique sur les rives du St-Laurent recouvertes de glace, entre Montréal et Québec. Au seizième et au dix-septième siècle, les Français y établirent les premiers forts et colonies.

Typisch franko-kanadische Kleinstadt am St. Lorenzstrom zwischen Montreal und Quebec. Nur eine schmale Fahrrinne ist noch offen im zugefrorenen Strom. Bereits im 16. und 17. Jahrhundert gründeten hier Franzosen die ersten Forts und Siedlungen.

Many areas of Canada like this lake
landscape in the forests of Northern Ontario
can only be reached by airplane.

Beaucoup d'endroits du Canada, comme
cette région boisée du nord de l'Ontario, ne
sont accessibles qu'en avion.

Viele Gebiete Kanadas, wie hier die
Seenlandschaft in den Wäldern Nord-
Ontarios, können noch immer nur mit dem
Flugzeug erreicht werden.

Jean-Louis Gagnon
Canada – Unity in Diversity

How many peoples took part in the discovery of North America? It is said that, at the beginning of the 14th century, the Vikings were already at work on the east coast of Canada. A hundred years later, the French in their turn took to the sea, while the Spaniards were discovering Florida and the Portuguese reached Newfoundland. In 1604, Port-Royal was founded; in 1608, Quebec. In 1609, the Dutch established themselves at New York. Then came English captains who left their names on the bays, lands and seas they discovered: Hudson, Frobisher, and Baffin. Just before the turn of the century, Louisiana was born. Meanwhile, the Russians were fox-hunting in Alaska and founding small farm settlements on the sheltered shores of California.

In all, the Europeans spent 200 years in the discovery of North America. But it took another 150 years before the United States and Canada assumed the definitive form by which we know them. In fact, it was not until 1867 that the Russians sold Alaska to the American Government; and that the British territories of the continent, except for Newfoundland, came together within the Canadian Confederation. Now the die was cast. Only France was to keep a foothold in North America, on the islands of Saint-Pierre and Miquelon. But something of this great adventure lived on in ferment: the shared determination of these Europeans of yesterday to build a new world on this continent, a world different from the old because it was shaped by new realities.

On a map of the world, Canada covers an area equal to that of Europe – that is, of a continent stretching from the Highlands of Scotland to the Urals. Canada abuts on the United States and stretches to the North Pole; it extends from the shores of the Atlantic to the Pacific Coast. Moreover – as if insatiable for land and space – it is anchored on two islands – Newfoundland and Vancouver Island. Only yesterday, to cross the country by automobile from east to west meant travelling part way through the United States. Today, the Trans Canada Highway allows the traveller to drive from St. John's to Victoria. But the road is so long that there is one "mile zero" at either end of the country. Yet this, the longest road in the world – 5680 miles or about 9500 kilometers – ends at no border. To the east, the west and the north, ocean lies all around. For Canada has only one neighbor, the United States of America.

At every hand, there is undeniable evidence of the weight of the United States in our daily life. While some regret this, no one could really be surprised at the way common habits link the five regions of Canada with the neighboring states in the USA. In what I call the "hand" theory, each finger has a name: the thumb stands for the Atlantic region; the forefinger, Quebec; the middle finger, Ontario; the ring finger, the Prairies; and finally, the little finger, the Pacific Coast. Travelling in North America, it does not take long to notice that nobody resembles a clergyman, a lawyer or a fisherman from the Maritimes more than a clergyman, a lawyer or a fisherman from New England. Austerity, diet, ideas of law and order and of morality, a similar relative poverty – everything demonstrates that here, geography, economy and way of life transcend the political boundary. In the same way, Montreal looks to New York as surely as Toronto belongs, like Chicago and Pittsburg, to the industrial basin of the Great Lakes. What we call the Prairies in Manitoba, Saskatchewan and Alberta become the Great Plains of Dakota and Montana on the other side of the border. And to cross the Rockies is to discover immediately that Vancouver, like San Francisco, shares in a way of life that is special to the Pacific coast.

There is, however, a difference in kind between Canada and the United States: the social and religious fabric of the population of the two countries.

Where do the Canadians come from?

A few have been there all along: 250,000 Indians, which is more or less the same number who lived in the country when the white man came; and 15,000 of the 60,000 Eskimoes who live in Greenland, Alaska, the Soviet Union and Canada. But the largest groups are descended from what we now call "the two founding peoples": 10 million of these are of British stock and 6 million of French. The "others" make up the third element of the population. We owe them much. The first to arrive, those who came with the original wave of immigration at the turn of the century, built the Western provinces with their own hands. Today, their grandchildren still maintain those prairie communities where people, driven by historic chance and persecution, strove to recreate little bits of Europe. By contrast, many of those who came after the Second World War – anxious to forget the past and determined to become full citizens like everyone else – were absorbed more quickly into the mainstream of Canadian life. They largely contributed to ridding the biggest cities – Montreal, Toronto and Vancouver – of their provincialism and in so doing, to making the Canada of today a North American nation. Because he invariably inherits a culture and belongs in most instances in a particular setting, a European does not have to seek an identity for himself; his culture and background normally provide him with such an identity for life. In fact, most people find it hard to change their identity – or, as the French have it, "to change their skin." Not everybody who wants to can become an Italian; and if it takes three generations to make a gentleman, how many must it take to make a Frenchman – even one who immigrated as long as 1640 – into a white Anglo-Saxon Protestant – a real WASP?

Since there are relatively few Canadians, they ought in theory to be as alike as brothers. However, scattered as they are in groups here and there over a national territory second in size only to that of the Soviet Union, they have, for one thing, acquired certain regional characteristics that only a substantial increase in the population would blur if there were a larger population, the relative isolation of the regions would diminish and Canadians would strike us as less different from one another. Moreover, Canada is a multi-racial federation with two official languages. How

then can the distinguishing characteristics of each of the cultural groups that have chosen to live in the one country possibly be found in a single representative citizen? Clearly it would be possible to conclude that, in such circumstances, any policy of national unity is bound to fail. Strangely enough, the question that arises, however, is whether attempts to create a single model of Canadian in the face of the United States would not tend rather to endanger the fragile foundations of Canadian identity.

This said, it remains the case that the average Canadian in 1976 is someone who speaks English or French, more often English; who still identifies himself with the part of the country where he was born; who looks on life as a North American; but who is convinced that his personal record-card is incomplete if it does not state his ethnic origin. Of course, there are Canadians who believe this determination to identify each ethnic component of the Canadian nation, and to count up their numbers at every census, goes against the very objectives of a consistent policy of national unity. But in fact, the opposite is true, since multiculturalism is one of the fundamental characteristics of our identity. Canada has never sought to be a melting pot, and it has never been the aim of our immigration policy to assimilate so-called "new Canadians." Simply fitting them in is enough to make them

84

good citizens. How, then, have immigrants succeeded – when they wanted to – in preserving their particular cultural features? This question comes back to what was the basis of French and British colonial policy in Canada: the role – or better, the mission – of the Church. No doubt we've changed. For some, this backward pilgrimage began long ago. But it is impossible to understand Canadians without appreciating that they were for generations the product of one theology or another; and remembering that in less than a decade – albeit under the influence of a Council – people in town and country lost not their faith, but the habit of identifying each other on the basis of religion.

Canada was discovered at the time of the wars of religion; it became a settled colony when it was the king's religion that determined the religion of the state he ruled. Since "national languages" did not yet exist in Europe, people did not understand that language could be a factor of political unity. In fact, neither in France nor in Britain did linguistic unity become an evident reality until the end of the 18th century. So it was not surprising that, when the Treaty of Paris was signed in 1763, it seemed more important to the belligerents, in accordance with the custom of the time, to guarantee freedom of religion to the French in Canada – in this case,

the practice of Catholicism – than to give official status to the French language. Similarly, it is significant that while Article 93 of the British North America Act of 1867 specifies that Protestants shall have the right to confessional schools, it does not say that the instruction in these schools shall be in English.

Whether consciously or not, Canadian immigration policy developed on the basis of this tradition: for one thing, because it was the way things were done, or the custom, but for another, because Catholicism – and with it, the French language – was no longer open to discussion. If the ministers of Cape Breton in Nova Scotia decided in 1713, after the Treaty of Utrecht, to preach in Gaelic, and if 200 years later, when the Royal Commission on Bilingualism and Biculturalism was established, Canadians of Ukrainian origin and Catholic faith argued that the language of their faith should be taught, and thus enjoy official status, it was because both could maintain, like Henri Bourassa, that since language was the guardian of religion, Canada could not be a melting pot.

It is never easy to define a people in terms of its institutions, for institutions change. And for a country which once saw the struggle for empire before becoming a land of exile or immigration, it seems safer to do so in terms of its geography and history. For a long time, the whole world was a European adventure. But in Canada, the British and French quickly eliminated their other rivals from the race. The confrontation between them was, however, to last almost 200 years. How could anyone have imagined – or hoped – that the Battle of the Plains of Abraham would mark the end of the French Canadians' long struggle for survival?

Norwegians, Portuguese, British and French – all of them discovered Canada. But only "the two founding peoples" wished to colonize it. John Cabot had already taken possession of Newfoundland in 1497 when Jacques Cartier entered the Gulf of St. Lawrence in 1534. Quebec, founded in 1608 by Samuel de Champlain, fell into the hands of the British for the first time in 1629. But then in 1696, the French burned and occupied St John's. Acadia changed hands nine times in a hundred years – a good demonstration of how intense the struggle was that began with the discovery of Canada.

However, when the British finally won, the departure of the French did not result in the departure of the 60,000 colonists who were already calling themselves Canadians. The struggle shifted at once to the political plane. The peace settlement had guaranteed the first Canadians their customary law and religious freedom; they were left to assure the permanent survival of the French language themselves.

Communities are shaped by their customs or laws, and by religion and language, in that order. From the outset, the customary law of Paris and the Common Law, Catholicism and Protestantism, and the French and English languages co-existed in Canada. For all practical purposes, Canada was the product of a new confrontation. This led little by little, through adjustment and compromise, to a balance, rare in history, which while thought-out, always remained delicate.

The Prime Minister of the re-created Canada, Sir John A. Macdonald, sure of his audience, said just after Confederation, "There are no more victors or vanquished; there are only Canadians." This Canada of 1867 was not sprung from nothing. It had taken living and learning under several previous regimes to gain acceptance for the idea of a federation where everyone kept his cultural identity and elected his representatives freely while respecting the rule of the majority – "one man, one vote;" and where there was the assurance that, under the protection of a self-governing provincial parliament, the French minority would remain masters of their own destiny. For a hundred years, Canadians of both languages often fought side by side to assert their control over the immense country they had only just finished conquering, determined not only to defend its unity, but to run its affairs as they wished.

As they saw it, only a federation permitted a sensible division of power between a reasonably strong central government and provincial governments capable of dealing with day-to-day problems and local matters. But it was also a way of giving French-speaking Canadians the autonomy they demanded. One hundred years after the symbolic deaths of Montcalm and Wolfe, the Canadian nation was born; the task that remained was to organize the country and give it a North American dimension.

The Treaty of Paris had granted the Canadians the right to run their collective affairs as they wished. This included keeping the French systems of land-holding and inheritance. In this way, the basic demand of His Britannic Majesty's new subjects was satisfied. (The same thing happened, incidentally, when Napoleon sold Louisiana to the United States in 1803). This decision was never reversed. For all practical purposes, it was again ratified by the Act of 1867.

In the same way, the new constitution involved – at least for Catholics in Quebec – the renewal of the guarantees they had received in 1763. Viewed against the background of Quebec society, it was in fact possible to look upon freedom of religion simply as an integral part of French customs. This was because the French Canadians had come historically to depend upon the clergy, to the extent the clergy had been obliged to assume certain responsibilities normally its preserve only in theocracies. This was the essence of so-called French-Canadian clericalism. How many career soldiers, senior civil servants, wealthy men, members of the professions, or sons of noble or ennobled families chose to remain in Canada after the English conquest? Of the former élites, only the clergy as a group chose to stay in the colony. That the authority of the clergy progressively came to extend to areas outside its normal realm was all the more understandable in that it represented an element of continuity at a time when all else was in ruins and only the will to survive remained. Thus it was not surprising that the religious question played a dominant role in relations between English- and French-speaking Canadians outside Quebec, particularly in Ontario, Manitoba and New Brunswick. But time would work changes. Anyway, it would not be otherwise, since Catholics now represent 45.7 % of the Canadian population, whereas the proportion of French speakers is only 28.7 %.

It was on the language question that the confrontation was sharpest. This was less true, however, in Quebec, where French enjoyed a guaranteed status, than it was elsewhere over the immense territory that all Canadians were coming to look upon as their new homeland. But the fact that, since 1534, French had always been spoken in Canada was to lead to the beginning of a long and patient policy of bilingualism for which no European model existed at the time. Two factors contributed at once to spreading French everywhere in Canada, and to inflaming the language struggle – doubtless because they were cause and effect. English-speaking Canadians would have preferred to see the use of French confined to the province of Quebec and to those federal institutions specified in the Act of 1867. French-speaking Canadians, on the other hand, linked the problem of the language – that is, of its expansion – to confessional schools. Once again, time brought change. Bit by bit, the idea of the French public school supplanted the idea of the religious school; and as English-speaking Canadians came to appreciate the significance of American investment in Canada (more than 50 billion dollars), they came to look upon the "French fact," as much as English political institutions, as bolting the door against "manifest destiny" – that is, against the doctrine of a supposedly "inevitable" annexation by the United States.

In 1976, few English-speaking Canadians would conceive of their country as one where unilingualism was natural. In fact, New Brunswick is now officially bilingual, Ontario has built up a system of education in French at all levels, Manitoba has restored French as a language of instruction, and in eight of the ten provincial legislatures, French is now an official language. No doubt the rights of the French language were contested for years. But it is nonetheless true that, since the Quebec Act of 1774, French has been a Canadian language even if it was not until the Official Languages Act became law on July 9, 1969 that "the French fact" came to be recognized by the English-speaking majority as one of the basic components of the Canadian nation. Professor Underhill has described elsewhere how political parties have served in Canada as a forcing-house for Canadian unity, at least at the federal level. It was within their national parties – and no doubt because the struggle for political power made it necessary – that English and French-speaking Canadians first learned to work together. Thus it was logical that the parties represented in the House of Commons should have voted unanimously to adopt the Official Language Act. One may say, therefore, that in varying degrees, all Canadian political parties today accept the obvious existence of what André Siegfried called a "Canada of two peoples," that includes strong communities of other origins as well, who firmly reject any notion of assimilation.

In its "Preliminary Report" of February 1, 1965, the Royal Commission on Bilingualism and Biculturalism reminded Canadians that their country is made up of two language groups. This concept is widely accepted. It is interpreted differently, however, depending on whether one believes in Canada as an equal partnership, bilingual, multi-cultural, and composed of autonomous provinces; or whether one takes the view that this equality requires first and foremost that Quebec assert itself as a sovereign nation and develop political structures permitting it to behave more or less as an associated state. But the fact there are separatists in Quebec as there may be in other parts of Canada is no cause for alarm. There are also separatists in Scotland, in Wales, in Ireland, in Galicia, in the Basque country, in Brittany, in Alsace, in Corsica – in fact, more or less every-where in Western and Eastern Europe. French-speaking Canadians constitute 28.7 % of the total population. More than 80 % of these live in Quebec. The number of French-speakers in the other provinces is more or less equal to the number of English-speakers in Quebec: more than a million. On a continent where there are 45 people speaking English for every one person speaking French, it would be unreasonable for the French-speaking people of Quebec to wish to cut themselves off from 20 % of their own group, thereby giving up buttresses in Ontario and New Brunswick, where about 700,000 people speak French. Not only so, but it seems clear that if Quebec were to secede, the result would be the break-up of Confederation. North America lends itself badly to Balkanization. In such circum-stances, it is reasonable to fear that the United States would weigh all the more heavily against the patched-up states that would emerge – so much so that Canada, dominated economically even more than before, would soon find itself at death's door. History's answer to the separation of Quebec, in other words, would almost inevitably be annexation by the United States. To sum up, the immediate aim of French-speaking Canadians after the English conquest was to survive in a distinct society whose laws, religion and language would be different from those of the Canada that was growing up around it. Later, they found in Confederation, which made their society into a self-governing province, a permanent political base in which they formed the majority. After a century of co-existence, the French-speaking people of Quebec want more. What? Two things: that the English-speaking majority should admit them first, to a share of power at the federal level, and second, to the management of the Quebec economy.

In practice, one might say that both the people of Canada and the people of Quebec wish to affirm their identity, the former against the United States, and the latter against the English-speaking majority. Both have simultaneously discovered the political, economic and cultural obstacles to doing so. For Canadians generally, the problems they face have seemed more than anything else to be a matter of their identity. For French-speaking Canadians, particularly those in Quebec, the matter has been one of survival.

Whatever the choice – whether it be federalism or separation – French-speaking Canadians are looking for life insurance against the growing risks of the future. Their concern has several sources. They were cut off from France in 1763. Initially, they established an agricultural society which was neither European nor American in its values, but which had the advantage, in the eyes of their leaders and of the clergy, of protecting them against any risk of becoming anglicized. How could anyone forget the call of "the voice of Quebec, half woman's songs, half priest's sermon" as it reminded Maria Chapdelaine of her duty:

> "We came here three hundred years ago, and we stayed . . . Strangers came around us, whom we were pleased to call barbarians. They have taken almost all the money, but in the countryside in Quebec, nothing has really changed. Nor will it, because we are a testimony – to ourselves and to our destiny. Because that is the only duty we have clearly understood: to hang on . . . to keep going. And we have kept going, maybe so that the world will look at us in a few hundred years and say: These people are a breed that doesn't know how to die . . . We are a testimony".

But life goes on and was to bring French Canadians to the Quiet Revolution. Inevitably, the industrialization of Quebec and the mobility born with the reform of education will have the secondary effect of making them more and more like other Canadians.

As the United States celebrates the two hundredth anniversary of its independence, many are drawn into comparing how differently things have turned out north and south of the long disarmed frontier. The truth of the matter is that, whereas the first waves of immigration into the United States brought thousands of men and women who were literally looking for a new world, the population of Canada was re-enforced from the outset by men and women seeking exile north of the border. French-speaking Canadians refused to join the Revolution in 1774 because they wanted to stay as they were. The first immigrants to choose Canada were the Loyalists, who also wanted to stay as they were, that is, the King's subjects. At the moment of truth, although for opposite reasons, both groups had chosen to be Canadian.

It is true that English-speaking Canadians, deeply attached to the British Crown, long refused to make any distinction between Canada and the Empire. It is not so very long ago that a Governor-General, Lord Tweedsmuir, had to remind them that the first duty of a Canadian was to Canada. That was in 1939. Since then, a lot of water has flowed under London Bridge. Among other things, Britain has joined the European Community. Today, what matters to them is to preserve the institutions of which the Crown is the symbol, rather than the Crown itself – above all, a Parliamentary as opposed to a Presidential system of government.

In one way, the existence of two language groups is at the same time the key element of Canadian federalism and, in a sense, its raison d'être; on the other hand, bilingualism and multiculturalism have greatly contributed to creating a kind of person who knows he is Canadian without being able to say why. French- and English-speaking Canadians have remained themselves, but not without borrowing from one another and finding many common interests: a taste for unspoiled nature and a passion for the wide-open spaces spring immediately to mind. But Canadians share the same attachment to certain more fundamental values. A sense of proportion, a respect for the rights of others, a willingness to compromise, and a certain humility in the face of their immense surroundings and of the powerful creativity of the French, British and American peoples with whom their history is inseparably linked, will be found in most Canadians; these are perhaps the most distinctive features of this still ill-defined people. If travellers in Canada often have the impression they are already in the United States, it is because there are only two countries in North America. European countries have much in common. Why should North America be different? This does not bother Canadians. They do not think they are being Americanized just because they wish to share the benefits of the technological revolution, enter fully into the affluent society, and become richer. Anyway, the same is more and more true everywhere in the world: the man of culture is the man who shares several cultures.

Because Canada is a bilingual and multicultural country, many ask if it will ever become a nation. Ernest Renan answered this question when he wrote: "What makes a nation is not speaking a common language, nor even belonging to the same ethnic group; it is having done great things together in the past and wanting to do more in the the future".

In other words, if Canadians were in future to act like the old nations of Europe, for whom blood has always been thicker than water, Canada would lose its point. But if they are to survive in the face of the Americans, Canadians will have to accept the fact that it is the very sum of their differences that gives them their identity. To exist and survive, the Canadian nation must obey the golden rule of unity in diversity.

The Prairies

The Canadian Prairies: their roads run straight to the horizon through a sea of land, flat in Manitoba, rolling a little in Saskatchewan, becoming hilly towards the Rocky Mountains in Western Alberta, interrupted only by a few cities and small villages.

Les Prairies canadiennes: leurs routes s'étendent à l'horizon à travers une mer de plaines, plates dans le Manitoba, un peu ondulées dans le Saskatchewan et devenant montagneuses vers les Rocheuses dans l'ouest de l'Alberta, interrompues seulement par quelques villes et de petits villages.

Schnurgerade Landstraßen, die im Unendlichen zu münden scheinen, führen durch die Prärie-Provinzen Kanadas. Die rot-gelben Getreidesilos sind aus dieser großen, nur von sanften Erhebungen unterbrochenen Landschaft nicht wegzudenken.

▷
Harvesting the Prairies' yellow gold, just before the first fall frosts set in.

Récolte du blé, juste avant la première chute de neige en septembre.

Weizenfelder – soweit das Auge blicken kann. In Saskatchewan, Manitoba, in Alberta. Ohne den Einsatz von vollautomatisierten Mäh-dreschereinheiten wäre es nicht möglich, die Ernte vor dem ersten September-Schneefall einzubringen.

Winnipeg, Canada's gateway to the West; its 2 large and modern railyards have made Winnipeg into Canada's no. 1 transportation and distribution centre for cattle and grain. Below: Grain elevators in Alberta on the transcontinental railway line.

Winnipeg, porte sur l'ouest du Canada. L'étendue et le modernisme de ses deux voies ferrées ont fait de Winnipeg le premier centre de distribution et de transport du bétail et du blé au Canada. Ci-dessous: des élévateurs de blé dans l'Alberta, sur la ligne de chemin de fer transcontinentale.

Winnipeg, Hauptstadt der Provinz Manitoba und Kanadas Tor zum Westen, ist Haupt-umschlagplatz für Getreide und Schlachtvieh. Viele Prärie-Dörfer und Getreidesilos liegen direkt an den Eisenbahnlinien.

Edmonton, capital of Alberta, was founded as a Hudson's Bay Company fur-trading post in 1795. Today Edmonton rivals Calgary as centre of Canada's oil industry and is the main junction for the two most northern highways: the Mackenzie Highway to Yellowknife, NWT, and the famed Alaska Highway.

Edmonton, capitale de l'Alberta. Fondée en 1795 comme poste de commerce de la fourrure pour la Hudson's Bay Company, Edmonton est aujourd'hui le centre de l'industrie pétrolière du Canada et le principal carrefour des deux autoroutes modernes du Nord: la Mackenzie Highway qui va jusqu'à Yellowknife, dans les territoires du Nord-Ouest, et la célèbre Alaska Highway.

Edmonton, nördlichste Großstadt Kanadas. Die Hauptstadt der Provinz Alberta ist Zentrum der kanadischen Ölindustrie.

Cowboyland Alberta: Rodeo and
Chuckwagon Races at the Calgary Stampede,
most popular annual event in the West,
attracting contestants and visitors from all
over North America. The oil centre of Canada,
Calgary is sometimes called Foothills City
because of its location in the eastern foothills
of the Canadian Rocky Mountains.

Alberta, le pays des cow-boys: rodéo et
courses en caravane à la Calgary Stampede,
la manifestation annuelle la plus populaire
de l'Ouest, attirant concurrents et
visiteurs de toute l'Amérique du Nord.

Rodeo und Wagenrennen im Cowboyland
Kanadas. In Calgary, Provinz Alberta, wird
jeden Sommer die berühmte Calgary
Stampede abgehalten. Eine traditionelle

Veranstaltung, zu der sich Teilnehmer und
Besucher aus ganz Nordamerika einfinden.

▷

A big country Canada needs big machines
and aggregates. Left: Open-pit mining of
coal. Right: Huge trucks are used in road
construction.

Un grand pays a besoin de grandes machines
et de grands moyens: A gauche: une mine de
charbon à ciel ouvert. A droite: d'énormes
camions sont utilisés pour la construction des
routes.

Ein großes Land braucht große Maschinen
und Aggregate. Links: Kohlenförderanlage im
Tagebaubetrieb. Rechts: Riesen-LKW beim
Einsatz im Straßenbau.

An Indian boy, smiling descendant of
Canada's first people.

Ce jeune Indien aimerait devenir un cow-boy.

Jimmy der Indianerjunge. Sein Großvater lebte
noch im Reservat. Er will Cowboy werden.

◁
"Valley of the Dinosaurs" is part of Alberta's
Badlands, a long dry area that extends into
Saskatchewan. The Dinosaur Provincial Park
near Brooks is the world's richest burial
grounds of prehistoric creatures, relics of a
time 70,000,000 years ago when Alberta was
still a tropical swamp.

"La Vallée des Dinosaures" est une partie des
terres arides de l'Alberta, une grande région
sèche qui s'étend jusque dans le
Saskatchewan. Le "Dinosaur Provincial Park"
près de Brooks est la région la plus riche du
monde en sépultures de créatures
préhistoriques, vestiges datant de 70
millions d'années, quand l'Alberta était encore
un marécage tropical.

Badlands. Vom südöstlichen Alberta bis hinein
nach Saskatchewan erstreckt sich eine
Wüstenlandschaft mit bizarren Sandstein-
formationen. Hier befindet sich der
„Dinosaurier-Park", die größte Fundstätte
prähistorischer Riesenechsen.

Duke Redbird · Alootook Ipellie
Indian and Eskimo Poems

MY MOCCASINS

My moccasins have not walked
Among the giant forest trees
My leggings have not brushed
Against the fern and berry bush
My medicine pouch has not been filled
With roots and herbs and sweetgrass
My hands have not fondled
The spotted fawn
My eyes have not beheld the
Golden rainbow of the north
My hair has not been adorned
With the eagle feather
Yet,
My dreams are dreams of these
My heart is one with them
The scent of them caresses my soul.

Duke Redbird

THE DANCE

The drum has started beating
The chanting
First high
Then low
And high again
The drumsticks are just a blur
Upon the painted buffalo skin
The chanting
A haunting cry
That stirs dead hearts
And moves deep passions
Abandoned down in the dark
Recesses of the soul.

I close my eyes
And darkness has disappeared
Color now is everywhere
Leaping and bounding
Laughing and swirling
Rising and falling
Spinning and curling
Rhythmically and symmetrically
The chant and the drum.

My voice and my heart
If they live
I live
Life and death
Love and sorrow
I am a man
And a god too
Joy, harmony and freedom
I am free and
I dance.

Duke Redbird

MY LODGE

Simple was my lodge of birch
Pure was the water that I drank

Swift was the canoe that carried me
Straight was the arrow that protected me.

Wild was the meat that I fed me
Sweet was the maple sugar.

Strong were the herbs that sustained me
Great was my mother, the Earth.

Duke Redbird

BANFF INDIAN SEMINAR

Like the wind that blows
The restless leaves of autumn
From north and south
From east and west
Four winds blow across this land
They 're called the winds of change
And they blow upon the indian breast.

They came . . .

They came from garden river and oshweken
They came from odanak and caughnawaga.
They came from many places,
With strange and common names
The cree, blackfoot, odawa, mohawk
The chippewa, abeniki, ojibway and sioux
The Indian sons and daughters.

And there beneath the mountain top
In the shadow of eternal rock,
The four winds of change
Fanned an inward fire
From the glowing coals of hope
That burn with the heart
Of the Indian Son and Daughter.

And these four winds
That blow from each direction

Have left a fire of hope
Within their hearts
That this Indian nation
Shall not be scattered
Like the restless leaves of autumn.

Duke Redbird

TOBACCO BURNS

Tobacco curls when touched by fire
The smoke rises – up –
Blue and grey
A fog that holds medicine
The spirit is strong.
The story is old
The smoke curls
I feel a sound – the sound
Of drums on distant hills
Of buffalo hoofs on frozen ground
A medicine chant wailing by breezes
That have not blown
For many moons; nor suns
That shine no longer on brown children
My eyes seek a vision –
For old people told of visions
That were not seen by eyes
But burned in the mind and mouth
Of our men

Who fought battles
But did not win.
My body cries for strong medicine
But my eyes water from whisky
My brain bleeds – my heart sweats
I regret
That tobacco burns
And I am not strong.

Duke Redbird

THE MARRIAGE

No priest had told her she was mine
No ring bound her to me
No ceremony had sanctified her soul
No paper had seen her name
Yet –
Loving hands sewed the beads on my moccasins
Shining eyes greeted me after the hunt
Tender caresses put my spirit to sleep
Silent words told me I was brave
For –
The Great Spirit had beheld her virtue
His voice had led her to me
Our Mother Earth received us both
We became one with their blessing.

Duke Redbird

LANGUAGE OF THE SOUL

The breezes rustled the leaves
The birds sang many songs
The forest moved in undulating patterns
The sun cast many shadows
The tall warrior who walked the path trod by many deer
Listened intently to the forest sound
For this was his language
This was not the language of sound
And only the soul understood
It was not heard but rather felt
Felt by the spirit that moved the man
Who had not learned the language but was born with it
A gift
Passed to him by others, that had borne it
    through these same forests
This man knew that the sound was from within and around
His camp-fire at night
He tried to imitate in his crude fashion
The story he heard each day
From his mother the earth
But his spirit was not the great spirit
His soul not the great soul
So he prayed and chanted for the day when he would
Journey to the stars
And he would leave for him who came next
A gift.

Duke Redbird

I AM THE REDMAN

I am the Redman
Son of the forest, mountain and lake
What use have I of the asphalt
What use have I of the brick and concrete
What use have I of the automobile
Think you these gifts divine
That I should be humbly grateful.

I am the Redman
Son of the tree, hill and stream
What use have I of china and crystal
What use have I of diamonds and gold
What use have I of money
Think you these from heaven sent
That I should be eager to accept.

I am the Redman
Son of the earth, water and sky
What use have I of silk and velvet
What use have I of nylon and plastic
What use have I of your religion
Think you these be holy and sacred
That I should kneel in awe.

I am the Redman
I look at you White Brother
And I ask you
Save not me from sin and evil
Save yourself.   Duke Redbird

MEMORIES

Wrinkles streaming down his face;
With eyes never to see again;
My grand old grandfather still lives.

With a voice so strong and wonderful,
He tells of the times when he was still
Young and fresh just starting out on
His own at the time:

He tells of the happy times he had
With his family, recalling his wife
And children together playing there
Inside the igloo and enjoying their
Togetherness in the isolated camp.

He tells of the first bow and arrows
He made, as his family watched with
Great interest, to make his day rather
Enjoyable working on the things he
Needed to get their food.

He tells of the time he went out with
Others on the lake to get some ice
When the rivers were frozen and covered
With snow, and how wonderful it was to
Help one another.

He tells of the summer he remembers so
Well when food was scarce and winds seldom
Calm; a bull caribou happened to stroll by
Their camp, and he himself stretched the string
Of his bow to let go an arrow through the
Heart that stopped, and once again fill their
Stomach where food was so low.

He tells of the wind that struck so sudden on
His return home one day, he had to stop and
Quickly create a dome of snow which was so handy
Waiting to be made.

He tells of the time he fought a hungry wolf under
The darkened skies when luck was on his side, for the
Chilly winds helped him win his battle; his clothes of
Skin had hardened like the ice.

He speaks so smooth and soft into my ears, that
I seem to dream with opened eyes.
Listening to an old man's voice makes me
Feel I am not wasting my time sitting
Under his chin.

Will these memories be
Remembered by the Inuit
People of the north?

Alootook Ipellie

THE DANCING SUN

There were times in the Inuit land
When the Sun would dance for us.
All the Inuit stopped their daily routines at work
And sat to watch the Sun dance in the Inuit way.

The Inuit would sit and admire the smiling sun.
The animals, too, it's been known, would do the same.
"I am a happy sun", he would say, "come dance with me!"
All the Inuit would join hands and dance, and dance, and dance . . .

The dance would enlighten the minds of the people
And prepared them to face the day in joy.
It was great to have a sun who danced for you,
Make you laugh, and have a wonderful time.

Sometimes the clouds covered the sky
So we couldn't see the dancing sun for several days.
But as soon as the clouds were gone with the wind,
The sun would appear again and say,

"Come dance with me!"
All the Inuit would come and dance in joy
With the dancing sun who danced in the Inuit way
In the Inuit land.

Alootook Ipellie

THE PASSING OF SPRING AND SUMMER

The wind is slowing down
After weeks of strong force
Through the barrens of the Arctic
The clouds are moving on to make
Room for the sun so its rays will
Touch the earth below
And melt the snow away
And streams are born to flow
Along the furrows of nature for
Spring and summer are here again
To stay.

Life in the North at this time of
Year is moving and filled with
New hopes for those who dream;
And for others, it is a time for
Continuation of a tradition
When one sits in the sun
And watch the children play.

The air around becomes tame
And goes along wherever you go:
To places where people work,
Stop and smile, then continue
With their work as you walk along
The sandy roads of the Arctic.

The days grow long as the sun
Climbs high into the sky and stays
Until the hour hand of the clock
Strikes twelve twice a day;
And people never want to go to
Sleep for darkness never comes.

The ice breaks up and there
Beneath open sea emerges and
People start to repair their
Boats and sail to the camps.
From there, they hunt the animals
Of the barren land to again live
As a band of Inuit
Living off the land.

The seasons of spring and summer
Pass much too fast here in the
North for we enjoy it
With our hearts
And signs of winter start
Creeping in from the sky above
And people start their
Memories of the past.

The wind of the Arctic sets in,
Cool at first, then chills as
The clouds move in and block the

Warm rays of the sun. The first
Snow flakes stant coming down
To the earth and cover the
Streams like blankets for they
Will go back to sleep until
Spring and summer
Are here again to stay.

Alootook Ipellie

THE TRIP NORTH

The North was the place you had
Decided to go to for your holiday.
For the Arctic was the place you
Had wondered about so much before.
So you flew up there and wanted
To find the very truth of it.

The scene was beautiful if you
Knew how to see the hidden beauty.
The color of the setting sun
Was most unusual in the world.
The bright and jumping northern
Lights danced you don't know how.

The wind was so strong at times
You wondered what will happen next.
The bitter cold was freezing for
A long time when you stayed.
The land was so vast and quiet
That it made you feel like nothing.

The snow was so deep that it
Covered your whole body.
But you stayed there until your
Holiday was over that day,
And flew back to your hometown
Where many people live.

You sit there at home and think
About the experience you had.
You agree to yourself that you
Plan to go up again next holiday.
Maybe it would be wise to be
Prepared for the next trip North.

You now read about the Arctic
In the comfort of your chair . . .

Alootook Ipellie

ONE OF THOSE WONDERFUL NIGHTS

It was one of those wonderful nights
When we gathered at the dance house.
I recall the familiar sights
When everyone laughed and danced
And had a tremendous time.
The great drums were booming,
Hands were clapping,
And happy faces were rocking back
And forth with the rhythmic dancing
Of the woman who had four legs.
Happy were those days when this
Woman danced all night long without
Resting for a moment.
She gave us so much joy,
So much feeling for life,
That the hazards of the land were
Forgotten –
In one of those wonderful nights
When we gathered at the dance house.

Alootook Ipellie

THE MIDNIGHT SHAMAN

I can scarcely remember a dream.

I was in a moonlit night
I saw an igloo sitting there
All alone in the middle of nowhere.
The size of the igloo was only
About one yard across the centre.
It had no doorway to get in or out.

I wondered what could be inside
Moving around and scratching the
Snow away. I had to find out.

I removed one of the blocks of
Snow and out came a young man's head,
Whose body was a lower leg and foot.
It was wearing the most beautiful
Kamik I had ever seen.

With a pale frantic face he shouted
Out: "The midnight shaman has come!
The midnight shaman has come!"
He dashed around me once and ran
One-footed toward the north and
Disappeared behind the hills.
That was the direction where
Ujualuk the shaman was presumed to
Have gone to die alone.   Alootook Ipellie

The Canadian North

The first Northern lights, shimmering
mysteries of the Aurora Borealis, announce
the long Canadian winter to come.

Les premières lumières du Nord faisant
miroiter les mystères de l'Aurore Boréale,
annoncent le long hiver canadien.

Mit den ersten Nordlichtern, die in kalten
Oktobernächten über den sternklaren Himmel
geistern, kündigt sich der kanadische Winter
an.

▷
Crude oil, most sought after mineral in the
world today, is found and exploited in the
Arctic and Canadian Northwest. For Canada's
North, oil remains the main source of energy.

Le pétrole brut, minerai le plus convoité, est
exploité dans le Nord-ouest du Canada et
dans l'Arctique où sommeillent d'immenses
réserves constituant la principale source
d'énergie du Nord du pays.

In den arktischen Zonen des Landes warten
noch reiche Erdölvorkommen auf die
Erschließung. Einziges Verkehrsmittel in
diesem unwegsamen Gebiet ist oft das
Wasserflugzeug.

This huge stone construction, Prince of Wales Fort, was built from 1732–1771 and was once North America's most northerly fortress. Partially restored, it is now preserved by the Canadian government, in a 50-acre historical park near Churchill.

Les Britanniques construisirent de 1732 à 1771 cette énorme forteresse de pierre, la plus septentrionale de l'Amérique du Nord, et située près de l'embouchure de la rivière Churchill, dans la baie d'Hudson. Elle joua un rôle important dans la conquête du Nord-ouest.

Fort Prince of Wales, erbaut von den Briten 1732–1771. Nordamerikas nördlichste Festungsanlage, nahe der Mündung des Churchill River in die Hudson Bay gelegen, spielte bei der Erschließung des Nord-Westens eine wichtige Rolle.

▷
Hudson Strait, passage from the Atlantic Ocean to Hudson Bay, bordered in the north by Baffin Island, in the south by the Barren Lands of Labrador and Northern Quebec: the harsh and somewhat monotonous mood of tundra and taiga, where the caribou is king.

La Hudson-Strait est bordée au nord par la terre de Baffin, au sud par les Barren Lands du Labrador et le nord du Québec. Cette voie maritime d'été relie la baie d'Hudson, immense mer intérieure, à l'Atlantique.

Die Hudson-Strait verläuft zwischen den Tundren von Labrador und Baffin-Island, Kanadas größter Arktik-Insel. Der nur im Sommer eisfreie Schiffahrtsweg verbindet die Hudson-Bay, ein riesiges Binnenmeer, mit dem Atlantik.

One of the world's largest non-polar glacier systems, the St. Elias Icefields, in Kluane National Park, in the south-western corner of the Yukon Territory and extending into Alaska. Mt. Logan, Canada's highest peak at 19,850 feet, is part of the St. Elias Mountains.

Un des plus grands ensembles de glaciers non polaires du monde, les St-Elias Icefields (champ de glace St-Elias), dans le Kluane National Park, au Sud-ouest du Yukon, et s'étendant jusqu'à l'Alaska. Le Mt. Logan, le sommet le plus élevé du Canada, culminant à 19 850 pieds, fait partie des montagnes de St. Elias.

Gletscher im Kluane National-park an der Grenze nach Alaska. Hier, an der Südwestecke des Yukon-Territoriums, reckt auch der Mt. Logan, mit 6050 Metern Kanadas höchster Berg, seinen immer schneebeckten Gipfel in den Himmel.

◁
The Hay River is one of many rivers that empties into Great Slave Lake, from which the Mackenzie River starts its 2,635-mile journey to the Arctic Ocean. Left: Indian Paintbrush, flower of melancholy.

Les chutes Alexandra de la Hay (109 pieds de hauteur). Cette rivière se jette dans le Grand Lac des Esclaves, où prend naissance la rivière Mackenzie pour achever son cours de 2635 miles dans l'océan Arctique. A gauche: une fleur que les Indiens appellent le "Paintbrush", fleur de la mélancolie.

Die Alexandra-Fälle des Hay-River (Gefälle 33 Meter). Wie viele andere Flußsysteme mündet auch der Hay-River in den Großen Sklavensee, dessen Wasser durch den Mackenzie-River ins Nordpolar-meer fließen. Links: „Indian Paintbrush", Symphonie in Farbe.

Left: Candle Ice, sculptured by nature. Above: Deep-frozen berries . . . the frost came too early.

A gauche: le Candle Ice, glacier en forme de bougie, sculpté par la nature. Ci-dessus: des baies gelées – car le gel vint trop tôt.

Links: „Candle Ice", naturgeformte Kristalle aus arktischem Eis. Oben: Eis-Beeren, eben erst gereift und schon tiefgefroren.

▷
Spring on the Yukon Plateau, the last treed frontier to the Arctic circle.

Printemps sur le Yukon Plateau, la dernière zone forestière avant le Cercle arctique.

Frühling am Rose Creek. Das Yukon-Plateau, landschaftlich dem kanadischen Schild ähnlich, ist das letzte Waldgebiet vor der arktischen Zone.

The musk ox, bison of the North: massive and archaic, the last horned survivor from the Pleistocene Age, roamer of the tundras. Musk oxen were always hunted by the Eskimo for their meat and soft, woolly underhair which was used for clothing.

Le bœuf musqué, bison du Nord: massif et archaïque, le dernier survivant à cornes de l'âge pleistocène, le rôdeur de la toundra. Les bœufs musqués furent de tout temps chassés par les Esquimaux pour leur viande, leurs longs poils, et leur peau.

Moschus-Ochsen in Verteidigungsstellung. Es sind die letzten noch lebenden Horntiere aus der Eiszeit, Nachkommen der Mammut-Familie. Ihr natürlicher Lebensraum ist der Norden Kanadas und andere arktische Regionen.

◁
Two generations of Eskimos, Canada's people of the North.

Les Eskimos, gens aimables et joyeux, vivaient autrefois exclusivement de la chasse et de la pêche, alors qu'aujourd'hui beaucoup gagnent leur vie grâce au pétrole.

Eskimos sind freundliche, genügsame Menschen. Während sie früher ausschließlich von Jagd und Fischfang lebten, verdienen viele heute ihren Lebensunterhalt als Ölarbeiter.

A. E. Johann
A European Looks at Canada

The word "Canada" is surrounded by a special aura in the minds of many people in the Old World. I myself belong to this large and quiet group who constantly dream of the immense Canadian forests, the thousands of crystal-clear lakes, wild foaming rivers and vast prairies over which ripening wheat ripples endlessly in summer like a golden sea.

Europeans' vision of Canada is not one that includes large towns. Instead, the image in their minds is always of green expanses, immaculate high mountain peaks, and the deep bays and gorges along the Atlantic coasts. However, Europeans have gradually come to realize that Vancouver, the largest city of the western Canadian province of British Columbia, is one of the most beautiful cities in the world, that cities like Quebec and Montreal are encrusted with the glories of history, and that their venerable and ancient city centres are just as "romantically" beautiful to visitors as the old towns in ancient Europe; and that this can be said as well of other cities such as Halifax or Lunenburg in Nova Scotia on the Atlantic Coast.

Nevertheless, for numerous Europeans, the extraordinary attraction exerted by the concept of "Canada" remains almost completely associated with the expanse, freedom, emptiness and overwhelming size of this great country in the north of the New World. Apart from the Soviet Union, no country in the world is larger than Canada; nevertheless, within these far-flung frontiers it has a population equivalent only to about that of two small European countries, Belgium and Holland together, and one of its ten provinces, Quebec, in itself covers twenty-four times as much territory as Holland and Belgium!

Put more simply, Canada has an abundant supply of what Europe so acutely lacks – space, wonderful unlimited space!

And with this space comes a wonderful list of possibilities, possibilities which a European no longer even dares to dream of, closed in as he is in his ancient part of the world where every cranny is already occupied and everything has already been done.

In places like Stuttgart, Göteborg and Padua it will be said, of course, that although the opportunities in Canada are great, the risk must surely be just as great! This is, in fact, a challenge which can no longer really be experienced in the Old World; a challenge which will attract anyone who is secretly proud of his courage and adaptability.

In past decades and centuries, many have risen to this challenge, this attraction, this exciting dream; they have opened up this huge land "a mari usque ad mare," as it is put on the Canadian coat-of-arms, "from ocean to ocean," and if we look at it carefully, they have done this in an unbelievably short time and, generally, in a surprisingly peaceful and careful manner.

Everywhere in Europe there is a yearning for a free, wide-open land in which resolute and capable men, unburdened by old prejudices and new confusions and entanglements can "begin again;" this yearning has increased even more since Europe has, with each succeeding year, more clearly revealed its internal and external insecurity and weakness.

I have deep knowledge of this matter. After so many visits and journeys to all parts of this great country, spread over half a century, and after many publications on different aspects of Canadian life, I seem, without realizing it, to have gained the reputation of having more knowledge than others possess of that marvellous area between Newfoundland and British Columbia. As a result, not a week passes in which I do not receive letters from unknown correspondents with contents I can surmise before I have even opened them. They not only come from Germany, Austria or Switzerland, but from more distant countries as well, and, on closer examination, they all have one thing in common; the writers' lives are threatened, or they feel that they are.

People who do not wish to be engulfed by unwanted or perhaps dangerous developments ask me whether Canada can be a safe harbor in which they can come to rest while there is still time. They also ask whether a daring and prudent man with special skills and a bit of capital – whether such a man would find in Canada many openings for a new existence? In Canada, they ask, would they find a life which would not be threatened by events beyond their control? Recently, I have received many letters like this from as far away as South Africa, from the former Portuguese colonies and from Argentina and Finland.

Each of these inquiries reveals a detailed description of another man and another fate. Only in rare instances is the motivating reason a youthful love of adventure or aimless restlessness. For the most part, my correspondents are nearly always "established people" who have already achieved something for themselves, who have seen something of the world and are therefore accustomed to thinking ahead.

I thus consider it to be my duty to give a word of warning to those who ask me about Canada, especially when they come from established situations in Germany perhaps or Switzerland; I tell them that while the conditions they assume to exist may, in fact, be basically true, they should also realize that Canada is an endlessly wide and young country, and therefore a hard country. It requires the use of all of one's resources and there are no safety nets available, particularly for the beginner. As far as I am able I also advise them to remember the size of the country – the fact that it stretches from the latitude of Rome or Madrid as far as the approaches of the North Pole; that what may be true of the "Atlantic Provinces," New Brunswick, for example, or Prince Edward Island, is certainly not necessarily true of the prairie province of Saskatchewan or the mountain province of British Columbia; much careful thought must therefore be given in advance as to where one wishes to settle.

Many of the people who have thought it worthwhile at one time or another to write to me for advice have in fact gone to Canada and settled there. Not one of the ten provinces was rejected by these enterprising people, not even the remote areas in the north, the Northwest and Yukon Territories. None of the people with whom I have kept in contact have given up. They found what they were looking for: freedom, space and suitable opportunities which they could take advantage of – in some cases, more than one opportunity. None of them have become millionaires, but all have found a new and secure foundation for their life, and nobody, neither fools nor the powerful, has disputed that what they have achieved is their very own. Many times the phrase "Canada has been very good to me!" comes up in their letters or during their visits to me. Can anything better be said of a distant, foreign country to which a person has entrusted himself?

Let there be no illusions about how difficult and remorseless this country can be. It is not the country for the weak or the timid, the lazy or the sluggish. You won't get very far there with the old kind of privileges of rank and position. I met a certain lord building a road; he was driving a huge bulldozer. In those primeval forests he was highly welcome and accepted, not because of his well-known title but because he drove the huge machine so well, operated it so carefully, accurately and surely. Nobody is expected, like a cobbler, to remain forever at his last. On the contrary: the person who is most highly regarded is the good all-rounder. This remains true, even today, during a time of general economic stagnation; those who do not get discouraged and perhaps even enjoy conquering unfavorable circumstances will sooner or later find their feet, will "make it," forge a new life for themselves and their family, a new, good home.

"Canada has been very good to me!" The truth of that statement is evident.

The threads which connect those who have emigrated with those who have stayed at home do not sunder; they sometimes last for generations. In addition, recent immigrants differ from early twentieth century settlers in two important ways – they have more urban skills and move into cities, rather than to the country. As a result, the image of Canada has changed quite significantly for Europeans. They have come to realize that Canada has its own national personality with highly individual characteristics; it must not be considered as just some kind of northern appendage of the all-powerful United States.

Only since the old ideas about Canada have been replaced by a truer picture has Canada been discovered by those people, too, who are not travelling because they seek a new home but because they love travelling and are looking for the many beautiful and bewitching faces of this earth. And now the word goes rapidly around that, in these days of the car, of fast railways and air travel, there is hardly another country so magnificent for travelling, for completely carefree journeying as Canada. Where else on this earth can one go over seven thousand or more kilometres continuously without stopping from east to west and without ever having to cross a political frontier with passport and customs control? Where else can one still have

such a magnificent, ever-changing panorama gliding by the car windows as one travels from St. John's, the capital of Newfoundland on the Atlantic, through Halifax, Quebec, Montreal, Toronto, Winnipeg, Regina and Edmonton to Vancouver and finally to Victoria, the capital of British Columbia on the Pacific? At the very best, only the Soviet Union or China might offer such a comparable experience. But who would, or could, travel in these countries, even if there were proper roads there – which there are not!

For in these days of unprecedented tourism we are gradually being driven to the conclusion that, if we ignore Europe, there is no other place on this earth besides the United States where one can give one's pleasure such free rein in viewing the wonderful landscape in the magnificently extensive regions over which the flag with the red maple leaf flutters.

We, of course, have long known that Canada can also be an icy land, a land of snow, of the shimmering Northern Lights, but in no sense can it be said to be *only* this type of country. The Canadian poet, Robert D. Service, speaks thus of the far north: "The summer, no sweeter was ever!" And he is right! When the ice has melted and has released the streams and rivulets with a great roar, the land shines with emerald green. The flowers blossom in abundance. The bees hum. The fish leap in the lakes. Wild geese fly north; in the silence of the magnificent forests young elk, deer and bears, beavers and lynx are born. The air is laden with a thousand scents. Pure-white clouds dream through the blue sky. A bird of prey circles high above. And it is warm, sometimes even very hot. And everywhere the clear pure waters, the rivers rippling silver over huge boulders, are an invitation to undress and bathe in the crystal-clear, cool water.

Thus spring spreads like some intoxication over the Canadian earth. But to keep men's feet firmly on the ground, to prevent them from settling into a pure sensation of well-being, spring also brings out swarms of buzzing mosquitoes and other stinging insects from the humid ground. Of course, you can protect yourself against them, and, as far as we know, nobody has yet died from mosquito bites.

In the hot, dry summer, this nuisance grows less and disappears in August to vanish completely by glorious September. The summer is a beautiful time! Then the endless prairies in Manitoba, Saskatchewan and Alberta show their full splendor and magnificence. The green, rolling seas of growing wheat are first gently pale, and then take on the color of red gold. As far as the eye can see – and it can see unlimited distances under the high sky in the pure, clean air – is an ocean of ripening, golden corn. The wind passes in waves over the corn and sings in the myriads of swaying ears, jostling against each other, singing a dreamy, tender and strangely melancholy song. As far as the eye can see, there is no human, no house, no tree – only the ripening wheat, this blessing of the earth! Far away on the horizon a few silver and a few red square towers glisten like small minarets; these are the grain silos at the nearest railway station of the Canadian Pacific or the Canadian National Railways waiting to be filled at harvest-time, when the powerful combine harvesters slice through the undulating land towards the horizon, gathering in wheat at each journey up and down the fields sufficient for bread for hundreds of thousands of people.

The summer is also the time when, in other places, such as Ontario, other crops like corn and tobacco, grapes and apples (of which a famous species bears the name of the Province of Ontario) also ripen; in the warm longitudinal valleys of British Columbia, especially on the Okanagan with its shimmering lakes, grow peaches, apricots, apples, melons, pears – whatever sweet thing the heart may desire. Anybody wanting to taste the most delicious cherries in the world, nearly as large as plums, and as fragrant as wine, should drive in summer cherry time to the furthest south of the Canadian Okanagan Valley, perhaps to Oliver, Keremeos or Osoyoos.

The year's abundance slowly comes to its end. The fields are empty. The fruit from the gardens is picked, examined, packed and dispatched. The colorful cattle, their coats gleaming, stand fat in the already yellowing lower reaches of the Rocky Mountains. The farmers sit down to draw up their accounts, working out in terms of costs and profit, the results of their past year's activity. And finally, after some beautiful, sunny, still and clear days, the first frost falls in the equally still night, and settles gently like a magic mantle over the country; all is silent, there is no movement of leaf or twig beside the stream which is the only thing which still moves, subdued and whispering. Even this is coated next morning with a narrow border of ice around its still inlets.

The summer does not yet, however, give up the fight. During the day the sun still shines warmly. But in the woods, above the river bank, the birch trees, aspen, willows, elders and maple have shown that they understand the sign of the first frosts, and prepare for departure. The pines, firs and cedars remain untroubled; they will not throw off their coats as will the careless deciduous trees which will throw themselves naked into the arms of winter after the riotous splash of autumn's color. They remain what they were, what they are, black, severe and impregnable.

Everything else green, however, blazes forth in the purple of the "Indian Summer." This is a festival which has no equal throughout the world, as nature bursts forth in all shades of gold from almost blood red to the most delicate yellow. The usually modest aspen are particularly splendid, and turn into sparkling, flaming torches at the forest edges and above the banks of the rivers which have been running for some time now with a sluggish flow.

This Indian Summer is not stingy, with its endlessly shining days; it is full of a fantastic and excessive sound, but laden as well with peace and melancholy. At no time is the Canadian countryside more beautiful than in these days of farewell. The insects are no longer a plague, and it is as though they had never existed. The heat, and often the oppressiveness of summer, is forgotten. The nights become cold; sleep comes easily. The days, however, are like wine, cool and warming at the same time – beautiful days!

Such splendor as this cannot continue forever. We all know that. Each starry night, the cold becomes a little more bitter; it is hardly noticeable but it can be felt. I like to think that I have always been able to sense in advance when the first Northern Lights would gleam in the sky, this entrancing flashing sheet of flame which announces the onset of winter.

I will never forget the night many years ago when I experienced a full display of the Northern Lights in the north of the Alberta prairie for the first time. I was travelling on foot – I no longer remember why – and I had some six miles before me in the

October night from the small country town (which in the meanwhile has grown into a busy centre of the then undreamed-of oil industry) to my somewhat remote quarters. It was a moonless night, but the stars were shining like twinkling diamonds, and provided sufficient light to illuminate the rough track. Although I was walking briskly, I was frozen. The day had been so temptingly sunny and pleasant, that the jacket which my host had advised me to take had seemed much too heavy for the warm weather, and I could not bring myself to take the bulky thing, which in any case I did not like very much. Then I had been held up in town, had drunk one whisky too many in the bar of the modest, always slightly dusty hotel, and had only set out home when the mercury outside had already dropped below freezing. I was quite aware of this, for the puddle in the pavement in front of the hotel door, which was always full of the water from the bucketfuls the owner had poured over the entrance tiles and steps, was already covered with a thin layer of ice dully reflecting the lamplight.

And that was why I was freezing in the thin, quiet wind, which cut across the fields, long empty and already ploughed, bordering my path which lay in a northerly direction. The slight muzziness from the alcohol which had spun in my head soon vanished. Although I still felt the cold, I began to enjoy my night walk under the high, sparkling sky, surrounded by endless space, solitude and silence. The song of the crickets, which during the summer had scarcely faltered, had long ceased. And then it happened, at first almost imperceptibly. At that time I was still young, somewhat arrogant I believe, and I was not easily impressed. But when the night sky was lit up before me with a strange eerie green, first very, very gently, almost unnoticeably, but finally indisputably clearly, I could not find any explanation for this fantastic appearance. I even wondered whether there could have been some poison in the whisky which I had more or less "enjoyed" an hour before and which had tasted very rough, strong and undiluted when I had drunk it with my companion – was it now affecting my eyes?

What nonsense! All doubts immediately vanished when a broad strip of light of the same, but much more intense green streaked obliquely and straight as dye into the zenith of the northern sky with such intensity of light that the stars in half of the sky were blotted out immediately as though in fear. I believed – and to this day will allow no one to persuade me otherwise – that, at the moment of this green lightning, which did not, like other lightning, vanish immediately, but remained fixed as light and hung in the sky, an utterly unreal crackling could be heard in the night which until then had been silent. It sounded like a warning of violently strangled thunder revealing its presence, but fading away in this eerie noise.

This extraordinary apparition in the middle of an apparently completely peaceful night so frightened me that I halted in my tracks. I stood and stared. Suddenly I knew what it was: the Northern Lights! My very first Northern Lights! I had expected them – but yet they were completely strange in their mysteriousness, in reality a true miracle!

The green beam remained for a time in the sky, a slanting, powerful shaft of green light, motionless. I was just about to walk on when the apparition disappeared again just as unexpectedly as it had appeared over the pale gleam on the horizon, as though extinguished. Was this the end of this nocturnal drama?

No! For from the high sky there suddenly unrolled a huge curtain straight across the whole of the northern dome. Vast green strips as though made of the heaviest silk hung right down from the zenith bunched together into many amply-rounded folds like the luxurious curtain around the stage of a theatre.

From one side, from the west, a wind from the spheres seemed to arise and began to move through the curtains of this phantom light, to make them billow heavily and loosely, billow and surge and roll in sky-high, continuously changing folds.

I stood and stared – and forgot the cold.

The whole magic performance then abruptly disappeared, so abruptly that I wondered whether I had actually experienced it. Nothing remained but the night all around me, a clear, cold night. The stars shone as though nothing had happened – and yet I felt that something really fantastic had happened. I buried my hands in my pockets. I was very cold; I had stood still for too long and I set on my way again.

But after only a few minutes the familiar green light shone once again before me on the northern horizon. I awaited the second act but did not wish to stand still this time. Arrows and beams of light shot powerfully once more over the dark sleeping land high into the void. The curtains flickered, billowed, yielded to the mysterious wind which allowed them no peace in their height. This continued for a while without the slightest repetition of any detail, paraded silently – no, at times with the very slightest crackling – before my eyes and then was extinguished in an instant and returned to complete darkness, as though somewhere in the universe a god of light had turned off the switch which controlled the flood of lights.

Shortly before I reached my destination, midnight provided me with yet another surprising variety of the arts which were unlike anything ever yet shown to me. After a fairly long period of darkness, the Northern Lights flitted across the sky again but in a different way. This time, yellowish and orange shades had mixed themselves with the pure and tender green which had so far dominated.

Suddenly the whole northern sphere stood purple

in flames, a surging mass of green, yellow, blood-red and gold-red shades, the furioso of a tone poem, its tremendous finale!

I slowly stumbled on, bewildered, indeed with a trace of fear.

To my astonishment I found my host, a farmer, outside the house when I finally arrived back five minutes later. I said: "I am late. I must apologize, John. But I am relieved to see that you're also not yet in bed."

"That's not quite true, my lad. We had arranged not to wait up for you and had gone to bed. But Martha woke up the same time as I did, and we both knew: the first Northern Lights of approaching winter. We just couldn't sleep through that. She's upstairs at the bedroom window."

I turned round. Yes, there she was, Martha Brinkman, my lovable hostess, waving at me. I could see her although the purple light had only just gone out once more quite suddenly.

"It's time to go to bed," said John. "There's a lot to do tomorrow. And, in any case, that purple light will probably have been the end of the fireworks. And it's bitterly cold. That will finish off the leaves. But at least we haven't missed the opening night of this season."

That was the first time I saw the Northern Lights. Over the years I have experienced many more, the most magnificent being in the north of the prairie provinces of Alberta, Saskatchewan, and Manitoba. God willing, they will not be the last. I have never been able to accept them as something ordinary or matter-of-fact. These mysterious fires of the northern night always enchant me anew. My breath is always taken away when, always without warning, once more they silently glimmer and glow.

Winter is never very far away in Canada, and tales of its severity still frighten many credulous people in Europe. Canada is a big, strong country; it stretches right into the regions of the Arctic itself, and it is true that its winters are great and severe – not the woefully half-hearted, pitiful winters of middle and western Europe with their drizzling dampness, their wet, rapidly disappearing snow, their grey weather which can never properly make up its mind to be either cold or warm. Although in Canada winter can sometimes be just as damp and miserable too; this powerful country is far too extensive for single concepts to apply to all its areas.

It certainly is the case that a real blizzard, a snow-storm, for example in the Dawson Creek area (where the famous Alaska Highway starts at mile 0) can strike fear even in the heart of a strong man. Then the world, sometimes for days, seems to be nothing but a horizontal sheet of howling snow which rubs against exposed skin like a steel grater, seals shut eyes and ears, and which threatens to knock you over like a raging torrent of water with a howling and roaring which swallows up all other sound. You just can't do anything about a blizzard like that. You have to bow down and submit, to bury yourself in the snow like the sledge dogs, who curl up together, bushy tails covering their muzzles, their ears covered, and allow themselves to be snowed over.

But no blizzard lasts for more than three or four days. Then it becomes very cold, still and extraordinarily clear with marvellously sparkling long nights; slowly in February and March the increasingly long days become so brilliant over the white expanse that it hurts the eyes to look at them. Over the long weeks of high winter the thermometer registers low temperatures, but each day remains as completely clear and still, and above all very dry, as the next. It may be hard to believe but the overcast winter days in London or Hamburg with their wet slushy snow which soaks the feet, zero temperatures, and dreadful wind from the west, freeze one to the bone more uncomfortably than in the completely windless stillness, utter dryness and spotlessly white snow of western Ontario or the Canadian prairies.

The Canadian saying, which I have often heard, is true: you have to say "yes" to winter because you cannot beat it. This saying has actually only come true since the existence of snowmobiles. On these motor sledges, warmly protected against the weather, the wilderness itself can be conquered, even in places where a summer passage might have been made only with extreme difficulty or not at all. For now all swamps and marshes are frozen over. The many thousands of lakes and rivers turn into marvellously smooth roads, and it is possible to go on journeys of discovery which could never have been attempted in the summer. It is therefore not surprising that the sport of snowmobiling has made a more lightning conquest of Canada than skiing ever did. Winter now entices one to rove into the glittering, white infinite spaces as much as summer tempted one into its intoxicating green.

But it would not be correct to allow this picture of Canadian winter to stand on its own; there are also other quite different pictures. In Vancouver, the large harbor town between high snow mountains and ocean bays cutting deeply into the land, the last roses still bloom in the gardens and parks around Christmas time – just as in the carefully tended gardens around the Parliament of British Columbia in Victoria on the great Vancouver Island. In Toronto or Hamilton on large Lake Ontario it is never really cold during some winters, and indeed one can sometimes wait in vain for snow – at least for snow which will remain on the ground. This is really not surprising because – and this cannot be pointed out too often – the southern tip of Ontario lies just as far south as Rome! And, although it stretches as far north as Alaska, the whole of Canada's Pacific Coast remains free of ice throughout the year as do the west coasts of Denmark and Norway. For just like the Atlantic Gulf Stream, the Kuro Shio in the Pacific keeps the northern and northwestern coasts of the ocean warm.

You can see, after all of this, that I really don't know which season I like best in Canada. Each possesses its unique attractions which the others do not share.

Exactly the same can be said of the magnificent Canadian landscapes. Let us name a few particularly characteristic highlights of a few of these. They all have one thing in common despite their diversity, the one thing which makes them unforgettable for any traveller coming from Europe with its small spaces, and that is their splendid untouched and solitary expanse. Of course, there are such places even in the most densely populated parts of middle Europe where one can still be alone with oneself and nature, particularly during the week, and even near large towns. But – and here is the essential difference – you are always conscious in the back of your mind that a few hours away, half a dozen kilometres further on, busy roads, railways, telegraph wires, villages almost within sight of each other, houses, people, hotels and factories stretch in all directions; one is constantly hemmed in on all sides by other people and human constructions. In contrast when I travel along nearly a thousand kilometres of the eastern section of the Trans Canada Highway making a huge semi-circle through the heart of the large Newfoundland Island, or if I travel along the Mackenzie Highway in the distant Northwest I may well meet no car for many hours of fast and smooth travel, and certainly no human settlement which could in any way be described as even a small village. Here the traveller is quite alone with the vast forests, with the shining, still lakes, and the monotonous murmur of the transparent rivers and streams. Sometimes when the Alaska Highway in British Columbia or in the Yukon Territory ran along the high ridge of a valley in which a river source sprang forth, and offered a panorama into the deep blue of the distance, I would stop the car by the side of the road and peacefully drink in the view. As far as the eye could see – and it could see into a distance which appeared to extend the horizon into the infinite – there were forests upon forests, mountains upon mountains; in the furthest west the faint outline of a silver tinge, the crests and firns of the high mountains. Solitude stretched away in green waves which took on tinges of blue and ever bluer shades. Here and there, would appear the faintest glitter, the reflection of a distant, probably unnamed lake – yes, far and wide not the faintest sign of human existence. Only wilderness and solitude as at the dawn of the world! And this vision can be found everywhere, even along the country's large highways. I have already spoken of the marvellous landscapes of Newfoundland along the Trans Canada Highway. I should mention the incomparable "Cabot Trail," the hazardous road through the coastal mountains around the north of the northern region of Nova Scotia. Like this, but much more extensive, is the splendid highway around the Gaspé Peninsula which forms the southern flank of the St. Lawrence Estuary. It takes a full two days to travel along it.

The Laurentides Mountains are also on the west side of the lower course of the St. Lawrence River, to the south of Lake St. John and the great Saguenay which drains the lake at the oldest habitation on French Quebec soil, at Tadoussac, into the St. Lawrence. The Laurentides also have their fair share of good roads which open up the heart of their forests' solitudes to the European traveller. And I must once more sing the praises of the Trans Canada Highway as it shoots into Ontario between Sault Ste. Marie and Thunder Bay (which has grown out of the older towns of Port Arthur and Fort William) around the north of Lake Superior! The views of the lakeside mountains, which at times tower up high and jagged over still bays enclosed by dark forests, and over the mirror of the ocean-like lake, will make any traveller pause yet again.

The roads into the north of the prairie provinces possess their own characteristic charm. I have never been able to escape their attractions. They run straight north through mostly flat faintly undulating woodland. Despite all the solitude which unceasingly penetrates them they are never, however, monotonous. The images they present change incessantly. Rocks jut out clumsy and huge through the mossy earth. In these endless, only scarcely populated landscapes of the Great Canadian Shield running in a wide radius around Hudson Bay – in these pathless areas with their innumerable lakes, rivers, streams, with swamps which are impassable in summer, with marshy forests of spruce, elder, willow and rustling poplars, and huge rocks everywhere – the mantle of plant life over the stony crust of the earth is very thinly spread and shows great gaps. The Great Canadian Shield forms the real centre of this huge land of Canada. It took a long time for east-west highways to cut through it, although it had been opened up for more than two hundred years by well-established canoe-trails. Over these trails flowed a fortune in valuable furs from the northwest of Canada to Montreal and Hudson Bay. Now these districts offer an extraordinary wealth of minerals; we have not yet discovered, let alone extracted, anything like all the treasures of this earth. To obtain these the loneliest roads strike north to Grand Rapids and Thompson, to Flin Flon in Manitoba, to Lac La Ronge and La Loche in Saskatchewan, to Fort McMurray, to Fort Smith and Yellowknife in

Northern Alberta and to the North West Territories. The Alaska Highway which cuts through the north of British Columbia and through the Yukon to Alaska has, quite rightly, already become world-famous.

On all these highways and even more so in the countryside away from them, the European experiences – experiences in the real sense of the word – a wide, gleaming, empty world which has remained untouched since the days of creation, untamed, undisturbed, of overwhelming, severe beauty and almost limitless size. Nothing comparable can be found any longer in little Europe. And the traveller from Hamburg, London or Zürich realizes that the word "Canada" must henceforth be a magic word for him, whose enchantment he will never be able to escape – or even want to.

To avoid being incomplete, I must add that the far west of Canada, more exactly the southwest of Alberta and the whole of British Columbia, constitutes the most marvellous mountainous country which can be visited in any part of our small planet. The most splendid parts of the Canadian Rocky Mountains and the possibly even wilder coastal mountains are accessible by roads, unforgettable roads!

But all the unique beauty and solitude of the Canadian landscape does not satisfactorily explain why no European who has once properly experienced Canada can ever banish the memory and the yearning for this great country from his heart. Further south, the United States, although its landscapes stretch without a break over the frontier into Canada, is not able, I believe, to arouse this strong and permanent response in the feelings of the European visitor. Characteristically, the word "America" has grown to have the same meaning for us as the USA. The Canadians, however, are not "Americans," but "Canadians," although their homes are just as much in North America as those of the "Americans." The Americans have wished to be thought of as something special compared with Europe. Every immigrant, every traveller, must be transformed as quickly as possible into an "American" and acknowledge the "American way of life." This is a reflection of the fact that the United States deliberately and forcibly separated itself from its European motherland and consciously broke away from it. This "America" wants to be distinctly different from Europe. In its "melting pot," all European characteristics must be smelted into a specially American amalgam.

Canada, on the other hand, has never separated itself forcibly from Europe. Quite the contrary; numerous families for whom "American" independence did *not* appear a desirable aim, who did *not* want to consider burning their bridges with Europe, turned towards Canada. Canadians attained national status only very much later than the Americans, achieved their independence and sovereignty only gradually and peacefully, after treaties and agreements, and have remained right up to the present more closely connected to Europe.

In addition, from the very beginning two European languages have always been spoken in Canada – and still are – French and English; German has also remained a living language for a long time, for example in the Lunenburg region, Nova Scotia, in the heart of Ontario and later in the prairies. Thus Canada has remained much more positively a colorful reflection of the Old World, was glad to remain so and was even – is today once more quite consciously – proud of it; Canada is pleased with European elements in its country, of the French, Scottish, English, Irish, German, Polish, Jewish, Ukrainian, Italian, Greek and Scandinavian mixture. And precisely because of this, it has enabled a unifying Canadian collective consciousness to spread through all the many, fondly nurtured differences. The effort to assimilate as quickly as possible into an overriding and self-righteous America disappeared completely. The European was, and still is, allowed to be a Canadian without having to turn his back on his origins, let alone having to disown them.

So it is inevitable that the European experiences Canada as another country, but not really as a foreign one. Sometimes – and the older I get, the stronger this feeling becomes – Canada has even appeared, and appears to me like a liberated Europe, a finally liberated Europe! What better testimony could a European give to another country in another part of the world on the other side of the ocean!

The Canadian West

After sundown at one of the many picturesque
lakes of the Rocky Mountains. Our picture: in
Mt. Revelstoke National Park, British Columbia.

Crépuscule sur un lac pittoresque des
montagnes Rocheuses. Notre photo: le
National Park du Mt. Revelstoke, en
Colombie britannique.

In den großen Naturschutzgebieten der
kanadischen Rocky Mountains kann man
wild-romantische Naturschönheiten
entdecken und seltenen Tieren begegnen.
Unser Bild: Bergsee im Mt. Revelstoke
Nationalpark (British Columbia).

Night camp alongside the banks of a leaping
mountain river.

Campement de nuit le long des rives d'une
rivière jaillissant d'une montagne.

Nachtlager am reißenden Gebirgsfluß. Wer als
„Outdoors-Man" durch die Wildnis wandert,
weiß, daß er oft wochenlang keinem anderen
Menschen begegnet.

▷

Left: The leaf of the maple tree, chosen
emblem for the Canadian flag. Right:
Takakkaw Falls in Yoho National Park,
plunging 1,200 feet deep into the Yoho Valley.

A gauche: la feuille de l'érable a été choisie
comme emblème du drapeau canadien.
A droite: les chutes du Takakkaw dans le
Parc National de Yoho.

Links: Das Blatt des Ahornbaumes haben die
Kanadier zum Emblem ihrer Flagge erwählt.
Rechts: Die Takakkaw-Fälle im Yoho
Nationalpark (British Columbia).

Man in the loneliness of the mountain world. Highest peak of the Canadian Rocky Mountains is Mt. Robson at an elevation of 12,972 feet.

Homme dans la solitude du monde des montagnes. Le plus haut sommet des Montagnes Rocheuses du Canada est le Mt. Robson culminant à une hauteur de 12 972 pieds.

Der Mensch in der Einsamkeit der kanadischen „Felsenberge". Höchster Gipfel der Rocky Mountains ist der Mt. Robson (3.953 Meter).

Scenic Moraine Lake in Banff National Park, with mountain goat and kid.

Le "Moraine Lake" dans le parc national de Banff, avec des chèvres de montagne.

Zum Moränen-See gelangt man nur in den Sommermonaten. Im Winter versinkt die Landschaft unter einer meterhohen Schneedecke. Rechts: Kanadische Bergziegen mit dickem weißen Fell.

▷
Dawson Y. T.: the Klondike gold rush between 1896 and 1904 brought nearly 25,000 fortune seekers into this northwestern corner of Canada. Today, Dawson has been restored as a living museum and has a population of little more than 1,000.

Dawson, Y.T.: la ruée vers l'or du Klondike entre 1896 et 1904, qui amena près de 25 000 chercheurs de fortune dans ce coin du Nord-ouest du Canada. Aujourd'hui, Dawson a été restaurée et est devenue un musée vivant où la population s'élève à un peu plus de 1000 personnes.

Die Goldgräberstadt Dawson erlebte ihre große Zeit um die Jahrhundertwende, als das Goldfieber viele Abenteurer an den Klondike lockte. Rechts: Goldgräber-Utensilien erinnern heute in der Museumsstadt an die tollen Tage.

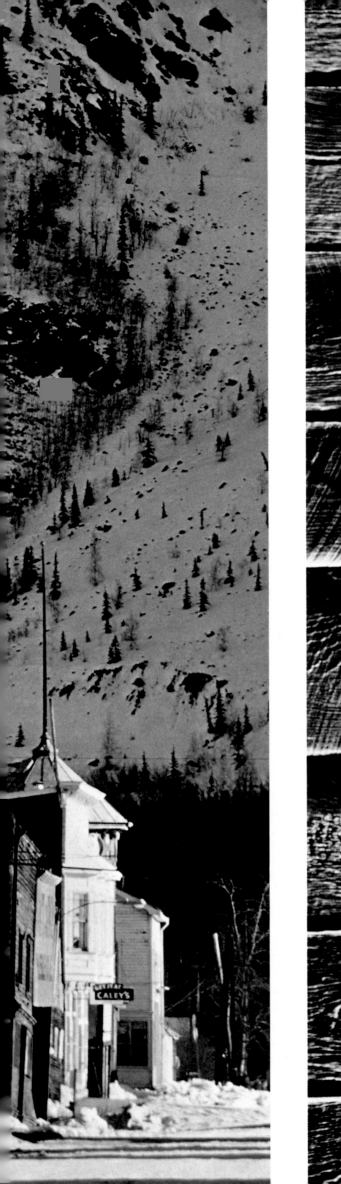

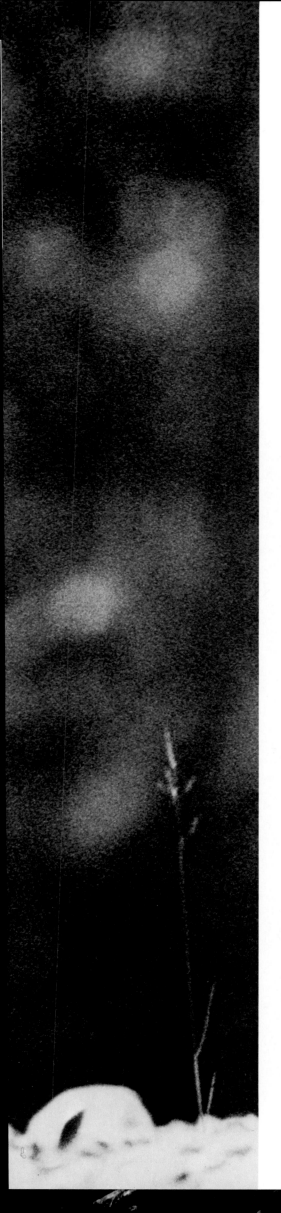

Black bears live in many large wooded areas of Canada, but grizzlies live only in the western mountain regions. The hibernating bears feed mainly on plants and berries, seldom on meat.

Les ours noirs vivent dans toutes les régions boisées du Canada, mais les grizzlies seulement dans les régions montagneuses de l'Ouest. Avant leur hibernation, ces ours se nourrissent principalement de plantes et de baies, rarement de viande.

Bären gibt es in vielen Regionen Kanadas. Schwarzbären und Grizzlybären sind im allgemeinen Winterschläfer und ernähren sich von Pflanzen, nur gelegentlich reißen sie auch Tiere.

Subtropical forest at the Pacific Coast near Alberni. Here, as well as in other regions of British Columbia are the cougar's hunting grounds.

Forêt subtropicale sur la côte du Pacifique près d'Alberni. Ici, comme dans d'autres régions de la Colombie Britannique, c'est le coin rare, où chasse le puma.

Subtropischer Urwald an der Pazifik-Küste. Auch hier befindet sich das Jagdrevier des nordamerikanischen Puma – „Cougar" genannt.

▷

The Indians of Canada have a great tradition and history. Indian tribes gather all over Canada for celebrations during the year. Left: The proud face of an Indian woman. Right: Co-existing monuments of Indians and European culture. Totem poles, the unique hallmark of the West coast Indians of Canada are symbolic sculptures with emblematic representations of animals and mythological beings, representing the hereditary mark or badge of an Indian clan or tribe.

Les Indiens du Canada se rassemblent régulièrement aux quatre coins du pays pour célébrer leur fête traditionnelle. A gauche: visage fier d'une femme indienne de pure race. A droite: des monuments de culture indienne et des œuvres de missionnaires chrétiens. Des totems symboles des Indiens de la Colombie-Britannique et du sud de l'Alaska.

Die Indianer Kanadas treffen regelmäßig in allen Landesteilen bei Stammesfesten zusammen. Links: Reinrassige Indianer-Schönheit. Rechts: Monumente indianischer Kultur und christlicher Missionsarbeit. Totempfähle, den europäischen Familien-wappen vergleichbar, gibt es nur in British Columbia und im Süden Alaskas.

Vancouver, third largest city of Canada ranks high among the most beautiful cities in the world due to its natural setting. The mild Pacific climate and long summers make this "four-seasons-playground" the "perfect place to live."

Vancouver, la troisième ville du Canada, 1,2 millions d'habitants, se range parmi les villes les plus belles du monde grâce à son site naturel. Le doux climat du Pacifique et les longs étés font de cette éternelle ville de loisirs "l'endroit idéal pour vivre".

Vancouver (1,2 Millionen Einwohner), größte Stadt von British Columbia, der westlichsten kanadischen Provinz, wird von Kennern zu den schönsten Städten der Erde gezählt. Schnee fällt in Vancouver mit dem pazifischen Klima selten.

A masterpiece of Canadian bridge construction, the Port Mann Bridge spans over the mighty Fraser River at Surrey, B. C.

Le pont Port Mann enjambe l'immense rivière Fraser à Surrey, B.C.: un chef-d'œuvre de construction des bâtisseurs canadiens.

Die „Port Mann Bridge" bei Vancouver, ein Meisterwerk kanadischer Brücken-bauer, überspannt die Flußlandschaft des Fraser River.

▷
Vancouver's exotic Chinatown, second largest Chinese settlement outside of China (next to San Francisco), with its own Chinese newspapers, markets, stores, restaurants . . . and telephone booths.

L'exotique quartier chinois de Vancouver abrite la deuxième communauté chinoise en dehors de Chine (après San Francisco), avec ses propres journaux chinois, ses marchés, ses restaurants, ses magasins . . . et ses cabines téléphoniques.

Vancouvers Chinatown beherbergt die zweitgrößte chinesische Gemeinde außerhalb China (nach San Francisco). Mit eigenen chinesischen Zeitungen, Märkten, Geschäften und vielen verlockenden China-Restaurants.

▷▷
Sunny beach life on Spanish Banks and Kitsilano Beach in Vancouver.

La vie sur les plages ensoleillées des Spanish Banks et de Kitsilano Beach à Vancouver.

Das milde pazifische Klima garantiert an der Westküste eine lange Badesaison. Bild links: Strandmalerei an den „Spanish Banks". Bild rechts: Kanadische Strand-Schöne am Kitsilano Beach, beides in Vancouver.